PRAISE FOR
The Graceful Exit

My family has treasured Mona Hanford for thirty years. For those who don't know her, you can little imagine the depth of her wisdom, strength, and compassion. Now, in the final chapter of her own life, when we should be tending to her, Mona has produced her greatest work for us - a run of wisdom on how each of us can exit this life with grace. *The Graceful Exit* is a book to be given to your friends and family. I only wish we could deliver to you Mona, herself. How she will be missed in Washington by the legion of us who love her.

David G. Bradley
Chairman, Atlantic Media

The Graceful Exit is a wise and wonderful guide to managing the most difficult challenge we face. It should be read by all, young and old, as a road map to a better way. Mona Hanford has been a powerful force throughout her life; this book makes her equally powerful in helping us confront death.

Alan Murray
Chief Content Officer for the Time Inc.
titles at Meredith Corporation

I have known Mona Hanford for over twenty years and I have never met a more dedicated advocate for the elderly and dying. This book raises issues that everyone needs to consider and discuss, and lawmakers need to enact. When individuals fail to heed the recommendations in this book, discord and disagreement often follow. As an elder law attorney for over twenty-five years, I have witnessed the positive results achieved by individuals who have proactively planned for death. Preplanning gives your family one of the greatest gifts you can give – family harmony.

William S. Fralin
Certified Elder Law Attorney (CELA)

I have had the pleasure of knowing Mona Hanford for all too short a time. In the face of her own personal cancer, she has demonstrated remarkable serenity, pragmatism with humor, and a continued desire to give aid to others. Her love of life and family is well balanced by her core belief in spirituality and the dignity of the human soul. Despite my 25 years of surgical oncology practice, I still learn daily from my patients.

Jeffrey Y. Lin, MD
Director, Gynecologic Oncology, Sibley Memorial
Hospital/Johns Hopkins Medicine; Associate Professor,
Department of Gynecology and Obstetrics,
Johns Hopkins University School of Medicine

Ars Moriendi — The Art of Dying — was a text written over 500 years ago that gave religious counsel about how to achieve a good death. Times have changed since then, and we've forgotten a lot. In *The Graceful Exit*, Mona Hanford offers us a personally informed contemporary version of The Art of Dying that takes into consideration modern medical technology, an uncertainty about religion that neglects the consolations of faith, and the human tendency to avoid what Hanford calls "the elephant in the room" — that death comes for each of us. In brief, accessible and lively chapters, this book offers practical advice about end-of-life issues that will change your death - and your life.

Donald Ottenhoff
Executive Director of the Collegeville Institute

As Mona Hanford faces her terminal diagnosis, she invites us on a heart-warming and thought-stimulating journey. She calms and challenges us. I hope you will accept her beautiful invitation to live every day with trust.

Anne Hisle
Bereavement counselor and author,
My House Burned Down and Now I Can See the Stars

The creative, comforting illustrations in this book by Lalie Tongour are a reflection of her talented, beautiful self. A devoted wife, mother, and community servant, her love shines through in her art. Ann and I are two of her most enthusiastic fans.

Alan K. Simpson
United States Senator, retired

This very readable book does an excellent job of "normalizing" a taboo subject in our culture. In sharing her experience with end-of-life issues, Mona speaks to us in her own voice so that by the end of the book we feel as if we have been partners in her journey. Her "God moments" make us reflect on incidents in our own lives that, if we didn't have a name for them before, we do now.

Barbara Rossotti
Former Board Chair,
Washington Home and Community Hospice

I love the conversational tone in this book. I feel like the author is right there next to me telling me that our end of life should be faced with dignity, rationality, hope and finally courage so we may accept our final journey with love, and not fear. We surely need to educate doctors and clergy to give us truthful options at the end, and to let us make our final choices in an educated and thoughtful way. I predict a bestseller.

Carolyn Johnson
Former Board Chair, Hospice Care of D.C.

People love this book! Like everyone who has ever known Mona Hanford, I am in awe of her passion and her brilliance. Her eternal legacy for millions of people struggling with end of life will be that she advocated for a graceful exit while she herself confronted her own end of life. This poignancy gives her book extraordinary power and reach.

Dee W. Nelson
Author, *Soul Strings*

Mona Hanford knows that dying well is part of living well, and she is a faithful, experienced guide. This most painful subject is handled with grace and humor as we are given the straight talk that is missing in today's conversations about death, because quite frankly, there are no conversations about death! If you need answers as to what to do when you don't know what to do–read this book. I can't recommend it enough. God bless Mona for being brave and loving enough to write it. May we all experience the love of God and family and friends she so beautifully speaks of as we each make our own graceful exit from this world . . . to the next. Peace.

Melissa Overmyer
Founder, Something Greater Ministries

Mona Hanford and Adrienne Hand have provided a template for a good death – "Peace at Last" – that will resonate for anyone whose faith tradition offers hope for life after death. Those without a strong faith will benefit from the practical guidance to accept that death is as natural as birth. Mona Hanford understands the real-world consequences of "doing everything," and using both head and heart to consider options for active treatment, palliative care and hospice. The tools offered in this book for clarifying and communicating wishes for medical, spiritual, emotional and social support when death comes near are the best I have seen.

Grant Grissom, Ph.D.
Research psychologist specializing
in coping with life-threatening illness

Perhaps Mona Hanford's book should be required reading for anyone over fifty.   While full of practical advice for those dying–and who is not–and their caregivers; more importantly, her work reminds us that the gift of life is a loan to be repaid at the end.   How we live this life, and how we approach that repayment, reaches deeply down into the heart and soul of who we are, and what our values are. Her work is not just about possible graces of the final passage, but a reminder of the necessary summons to courage, realism, spiritual risk, and humility it asks of us.

James Hollis, Ph.D.
Jungian analyst and author

The Graceful Exit
10 Things You Need to Know

*Face Reality, Make Wise Choices
and Find Hope at the End of Life*

Mona Hanford
AND
Adrienne Hand

*DESIGNED AND ILLUSTRATED
BY*

Lalie C. Tongour

COPYRIGHT © 2018

For my grandfather, Archbishop Amvrossy,
my role model for resilience, optimism and faith,
and for my children, Troy, Tania and Carter, and my
grandchildren, Alexis, Haley, Ford, Lainey,
Liam and Troy. They are my legacy.

Mona Hanford

MONA HANFORD

The author enjoying a peaceful moment
with her dogs, Ace and Liberty.

About the Author

Mona Hanford is the founder of The Hope Initiative, a five-part course designed to encourage and support caregivers, the chronically or terminally ill, and anyone contemplating life and its meaning. The material is faith based but will help people from all backgrounds prepare for the spiritual and emotional struggles they may face while confronting deeper questions of life, and death.

An eldercare activist, consultant, speaker and writer who has been working on end-of-life care issues for decades, Mona has been quoted and referenced widely in books focused on end-of-life care, and also in books with broader appeal. She was the expert cited in *The Seven Pearls of Financial Wisdom* for the chapter "Legacy Building."

Mona has been interviewed about end-of-life care issues by media outlets including PBS. Her 2017 interview on "Hope at the End" was published by the Collegeville Institute, and posted at Harvard University's Initiative on Health Religion and Spirituality, and Duke University Divinity School.

In 2001, for "The Journey of the Soul – Peace at Last," a sold-out conference at the Washington National Cathedral, she chaired and recruited 10 end-of-life care agencies as co-sponsors. 1500 participants attended and 500 were on the wait list.

Mona has worked with non-profit organizations for four decades, successfully completing 25 capital campaigns. She was concurrently Director of Development at St. Patrick's Episcopal Day School in Washington, D.C. and President of Elixir Inc., a consulting firm serving churches by conducting feasibility studies and providing advice on raising funds and directing capital campaigns. At St. Patrick's she directed all advancement activities including strategic planning, public relations, publications, special events and fundraising.

A networker and team builder, Mona has served on the boards of Capital Care and The Washington Home and Community Hospices, and the Collegeville Institute for Ecumenical and Cultural Research, among many others.

Contents

About the Author xi

Foreword by William H. Frist, MD xv

Introduction by Mona Hanford xvii

Chapter 1   Embrace the Elephant in the Room 1

Chapter 2   Death is a Spiritual Journey........................ 13

Chapter 3   Five Wishes 23

Chapter 4   Redefine "Doing Everything"......................41

Chapter 5   Seek the Comforts of Hospice..................... 49

Chapter 6   Be Open to Modern Medicine 57

Chapter 7   Plug Into Love 63

Chapter 8   Say and Do the Important Things Now 69

Chapter 9   Open the Door to God 77

Chapter 10 Embrace the Next Chapter 83

Acknowledgments... 87

Appendix 89

Beyond the Horizon: A Letter from Mona Hanford 93

Resources for Preparing Your Living Will.................... 95

Caregiver Resources.. 97

Foreword

As a physician and former legislator, I have been championing a revolution in end-of-life care. The way we think and talk about end of life needs to change. Palliative care and hospice should be incorporated into our evolving healthcare landscape. Mona Hanford embraces these issues and brings her experience and compassion as a caregiver, an advocate, and a patient to this important book. She shares her pragmatic approach to facing the inevitable and preparing for a graceful exit and a lasting legacy.

End-of-life care is perhaps one of the most complex, emotional, and delicate issues in all of health care. Those final weeks and months can be an incredibly challenging and, too frequently, confusing period for us. At a time when we hope for peace, tranquility, and dignity, a patient is often pulled in opposing directions by doctors, intensive care unit treatment options, family and friends, and by the demands of one's own — at times excruciating — physical pain and stubborn defiance of the natural process of dying.

My perspective comes as a surgeon who by the nature of my specialties of heart disease and cancer has walked with hundreds of patients and their families through these final days of life. It is never easy.

Advancing end-of-life care should begin in the living rooms of patients and their families and extend to nurses' and doctors' offices, hospitals, religious institutions, and policy chambers.

"How do I want to die?" That's the framing question. It's a tough place to start, but grounds the discussion in the reality that unless we act, our final days will be spent very differently than we would like.

Many doctors, especially those trained more than a decade or two ago, have had no guidance on when and how to talk with patients about the end of life. We were trained only to prolong life, not help in its end. Our focus has been on quantity of life, not quality of life.

Patients also avoid the topic. In a 2005 AARP survey of Massachusetts residents over age 50, nearly 90 percent said they wanted honest answers from doctors, but fewer than 20 percent had discussed their end-of-life wishes with their physicians.

Mona Hanford is a distinguished eldercare activist, consultant and speaker. In this book, she expertly discusses the ten things you need to know to navigate the inevitable with hope and grace. In sharing her story along with the stories of others and current research, she offers invaluable support and guidance for individuals and their families facing those hard conversations. Mona gives all of us the impetus to envision a graceful exit.

Health care is complex. I am working within the medical community to increase the options for end-of-life care, but it is up to us all as individuals to initiate conversations about end-of-life wishes with our families.

Thanks to Mona Hanford, this book describes death and dying with humor and steadfast faith that the Best is yet to come. A graceful exit, indeed.

William H. Frist, MD

Dr. William H. Frist is a nationally acclaimed heart transplant surgeon, former U.S. Senate Majority Leader, the chairman of Hope Through Healing Hands and Tennessee SCORE, professor of surgery, co-founder of Aspire Health, and author of six books. Learn more about his work at BillFrist.com. Nashville, Tennessee 2018.

Introduction

I have written this book as a forthright and compassionate guide for you and your caregivers, to help you make wise choices at the end of life. I'm going to give it to you straight. Yes, make sure you or your beloved family member gets the best medical care possible, but don't get caught up in fantasy. Medical science has come a long way, but it has not yet eradicated death or the slow decline imposed by so many diseases. Taking care of my husband and parents at their end of life, being present and advocating for palliative care for them and for friends during the long last chapter, and now, as I face my own cancer diagnosis, I am keenly aware of what matters most - and the best ways to plan a graceful exit for yourself and for those you love most dearly.

Too often today patients are left on the medical treadmill. The common reaction of family when hearing a serious diagnosis is to "do everything" to keep our loved ones alive. But beware of what you wish for... so many patients suffer in great pain in their last weeks and months.

To do everything for our loved ones in the end means that we must be sure they get care for the body but more importantly for the soul. I believe spiritual lifelines offer real hope. We need to look beyond the earthly horizon, and beyond the last acts of cremation or being laid out, embalmed and buried in the coffin and the dirt.

Dr. Carl Jung, the eminent psychologist, had this carved, in Latin, over the front door of his house in Zurich:

"Bidden or not bidden, God is present."

Sadly, many of us have lost touch with God and an understanding of the natural order. We all die. As Einstein said: "Genius has limits."

A friend once said to me, "Mona, you don't believe in God, do you? You went to college, you are educated, you know better." Well, having cared for my disabled husband Bill for eight years, I do believe. I could not have made the long journey by his side and been a witness to his dying in a hospital bed in our family room had I not anchored on the Serenity Prayer:

"God, grant me the serenity to accept the things I cannot change, the courage to change the things I can, and the wisdom to know the difference."

I did the best I could and trusted God.

Whether or not you go to church, you are a spiritual person. We all have beliefs and values that connect us to a deeper meaning of life. Some of us have a deep faith in the God of our choosing, be that the Spirit, the Light, a Higher Power, or whatever faith gives us hope and peace. Some of us refresh our spirit in nature, or strolling through an art gallery, or listening to great music. And we can all strengthen our spiritual life by spending time in quiet reflection or prayer. Prayer is known to bring a sense of calm and stability in hard times.

Caring for my husband Bill in his long last chapter, I felt like I was on a spiritual journey. Bill had a deformed leg since childhood. At age 61, he had an 11-hour surgery to straighten his leg. But the weak cartilage around his knee was still a problem. He had to wear a brace from the ankle to the hip. But the worst part was that during surgery, the 11 hours under general anesthesia triggered the onset of multiple health consequences. I thought he was going to die then, but he lived another eight years.

At age 71, when my husband lay dying in our family room, I received a card that said, "Do not fear, only Believe." I kept that card close by as my compass. I feel so blessed to have God in my life. During those dark and frightening times, I felt God's mercy and grace through the kindness and care of those He sent to help my family along our path.

While writing this book, a month before I got my diagnosis, I was sitting at my computer and I felt God's presence next to me. I had a conversation with Him right then and there. He said, "Mona, you have a very busy and full life. You work hard every day; you're advocating for hospice care and you're planning workshops to bring God into the lives of those who are most vulnerable. You're in the pool at the Y doing water aerobics, you walk the dogs down to the creek, you go to Bible study and church, and you visit with family and friends. You play on a Bridge Swiss team, you just planned a dinner with college classmates to support your friend whose grandson was just killed in a tragic bike accident. You're a busy girl. You need a co-author for your book."

That was a God moment. And the perfect co-author fell into my hands. No accident. God's hand at work.

When I found out I had cancer, I encountered endless inefficiencies in the hospital system. I could not reach doctors or make appointments. I got differing advice. And so I fought the health care system to get information – so I could make wise choices. Eventually, I got the expert advice I needed, but it didn't come from the usual channels.

Fortunately, God sends people into our lives. It was dear friends who brought me the help I needed. When I first started feeling unwell, I had called my OB/GYN practice that I'd been going to for over 40 years and they'd suggested I either go to the ER or take an appointment 3 weeks later. So, it wasn't my own doctor, but my son's best friend from high school who had become a doctor, who found my surgeon and held my hand at the hospital. He's the one who told me when it was time to go to the ER.

God does have a sense of humor. Here I am, living the book I'm writing.

There have been many God moments. Several months before my diagnosis, my water aerobics teacher at the YMCA suggested that I meet another one of her students, Ann Hisle. Well, Ann is the author of the remarkable book *My House Burned Down and Now I Can See the Stars*. Her book has been so helpful to me as I face serious health challenges. I call this God's hand at work.

When I have visited friends in their homes during their hospice care, I've always brought cookies - hot from the oven. I remember the look on my friend's face as he enjoyed this simple pleasure in the recliner in his living room. We sat together, he and his wife and I, and we prayed. How thankful we were that we had God in our life, and how hard this chapter would be if we didn't.

When a dear friend lost her grandson in a tragic biking accident, my college friends gathered around my table sharing food and memories - soul food. It was community that sustained my friend's son's family, as well. God made sure their house was never empty. Everyone came with food, flowers and hugs. That community kept them surrounded. They could not have survived without that outpouring of love.

Last week while I was cleaning, I found a card from my husband Bill. On the cover is a picture of an ugly bulldog, and it says, "Just remember - when life gets ugly..." and on the inside, it says, "...you have God and me in your corner." How wonderful to find that just when I needed to know Bill was near.

I was encouraged to write this book to share what I have learned about designing a graceful exit, "a good death." Finding time to do simple things with people you love. Looking through old family photo albums. Sharing meals with family and dear friends. Blowing bubbles with grandchildren.

Knowing God is by my side has given me remarkable calm as I face my serious cancer diagnosis. In practical terms, my body has functioned well. I had major surgery which left me with a 9-inch scar, and yet I left the hospital after just two days without pain pills or drugs for anxiety or depression. The doctors marvel at my resilience.

Though I am stunned that this happened while I was flying high in my life, and everything seemed to be coming together beautifully - family, friendships, my work and my mission - I am grateful that I haven't been battling cancer for the last 5, 10, or even 20 years, as some of my dear friends have. I've had a wonderful life for three quarters of a century! And I am reveling in the loving support of family and friends.

I attribute my emotional equilibrium and my physical fortitude to my deep faith in a loving God and to the love and support of my friends and family. A young neighbor has created an online sign-up for meals and visits. Friends bring food and fellowship. We eat and pray, and yes — laugh.

For 20 years, I have been counseling friends with serious health problems to face the reality that we are mortal. I have been a strong advocate for hospice care, which is comfort care and pain relief set up in a hospital room or at home when one is expected to have 6 months or less to live. This has often been unwelcome advice. My friends have said to me things like, "You have to understand. Mother is 95. She has been in and out of the hospital the last six months – but she is not dying yet. We have the best doctors. No one has mentioned death."

I am shocked that death is a word rarely used in hospitals. My very skilled Chinese surgeon once asked me, "What is it about Americans that they do not understand aging and death? Here it is all about looking young."

When we fight a debilitating disease, if we stay in battle mode beyond any hope for a cure, we are denying our mortality. This has serious consequences that we as a society need to remedy.

Dixcy Bosley-Smith, a clinical hospice nurse liaison who has been a hospice advocate and nurse for 30 years, told me recently that patients at a local hospital are not being referred to hospice until just days before their last breath, and by then the idea of hospice is a terrible shock and crisis for the family. Delaying hospice care, which is often delaying comfort care and pain relief, not only allows unnecessary physical pain to persist but, just as tragically, it severs our spiritual lifelines. When we are hooked up to tubes and machines, or on life support, there is little to no chance for us to connect meaningfully with the ones we love – or to have peaceful moments with God.

Hospice is a key part of a graceful exit because once our pain is lessened and we have an experienced support system in place, we feel better and we can talk with our family and friends. We can have those conversations that bring much needed nourishment for the soul. We can be part of a very special community of caring that surrounds you when you have accepted you are dying. This community is surrounding me now, and I am relishing the love and laughter.

Hospice is a key part of a graceful exit because once our pain is lessened and we have an experienced support system in place, we feel better and we can talk with our family and friends.

And yet many people, including pastors and chaplains, find it difficult to give up on invasive treatments. We talk about this more in chapter 4, "Redefine 'Doing Everything'." People don't want to hear that a cure isn't possible. Some hold out for a miraculous medical cure, sent by God.

People who are dying don't need false hope and painful treatments that bring suffering and may even hasten their death. They need to feel the love of God right next to them in their hospital bed. But they are often too sick to ask for it. Ministers or chaplains need to just come and sit next to us, and pray. This simple act is enormously comforting. Surgeons who pray with their patients before surgery offer much hope and relief from intense fear.

God's love and mercy are central to my life. They give me hope as I face my own mortality, and I want to spread the Good News. I am committed more than ever to spreading hope to patients and their families.

In 2015, I founded The Hope Initiative, a five-part course that is being given in hospitals and churches for caregivers. This has been a spiritual lifeline for many people. During each class, Reverend Jamie Haith of the wonderful Holy Trinity Church in McLean, Virginia shares stories of hope and God's love at the end of life. In each class, you are surrounded with the message of hope: that there is more after we leave this earth, and that we are not alone.

Like all of us, I want to live as long and as well as I can. I love my life! I love my family and friends, who have been incredible sources of love and support. The community building that I have done all my life for churches and schools and as a hospice advocate has brought me to a place of deep connection and gratitude.

My first chemo treatment yesterday went well, and this weekend I am going to be at my granddaughter's squash tournament cheering her on. Nevertheless, whenever my exit comes, my faith will sustain me as I say goodbye to those I love. There will be Peace at Last. I do not know what Heaven looks like, but I am open to the mystery of God's love. I am an optimist!

Knowing it is not all up to me, a mere human, to control fate, I can look out my window at the birds and smile when I feel the sun on my face. I can hold my little dog Liberty in my lap and know, deep in my heart,

"The Best is yet to come!"

Embrace the elephant . . .

. . . this is step one to a graceful exit.

CHAPTER 1

EMBRACE THE ELEPHANT IN THE ROOM

Come to Terms with the Reality of Your Situation and Navigate your Best Medical Treatment

Genius has limits.
- Albert Einstein

It is healthy and right to want to live for another day, another holiday, another hug... but we all have an expiration date. We're all going through the same experience.

We all live, as fully as we can, and then we all die. No one's going to buy a lottery ticket that will magically keep us here. People with terminal illness have a deep hunger to talk about and to understand death, but "it's not polite to talk about it."

Death is the big elephant in the room.

Even when a loved one is in hospice care, many hospice nurses have told me that family members will pull them aside and say, "Don't mention death to mother, whatever you do. It will kill her." And then the mother will pull the nurse close to her and say, "Honey, I'm dying. Do not tell my children. It will kill them."

Although facing death is a scary and difficult prospect, not facing your situation can be even more scary and difficult for you and those who love and care for you.

When we say, "I'm fine, everything's fine; my mother is not dying" to those who can see that everything is definitely not fine, we are shutting the door to love and support at a time when we need them most. Even more importantly, when we say, "I've got this. I don't need any help," we are shutting the door on God and any hope for a graceful exit for our loved one.

In Dr. Bernie Siegel's book, *Love, Medicine and Miracles*, he writes, "Lies and evasions drive family apart just when they most need to be united in facing the crisis."

Embrace the elephant in the room. And bring God in. Whatever your spiritual practice, now is the time to ask for God's presence and guidance. Let's face the elephant in the room. What if we could actually see and come to accept that death is imminent, and in fact, inevitable? Though this is terrifying, there is hope.

A wise friend said to me, "Don't worry I will be there when you get wobbly knees." She helped me to be the kind of brave[1] I wanted to be as I faced my own diagnosis of stage IV cancer and the unknown next chapter.

---

1. From *Be the Kind of Brave You Wanted to Be: Prose Prayers and Cheerful Chants against the Dark* by Brian Doyle.

God's promise to us is,
"Be still and know that I am here with you."[2]

When we put hope in technology and medications rather than in God, we feel a tremendous weight of responsibility, and we feel increasingly sad and hopeless as we look at an endless list of tasks that we fear won't ever entirely improve anything. Yes, we must do what we can medically. But God gave us certain gifts and we are to use them: our brains, our energy, resilience, and hope. So, do what you can – and then let go of what you cannot control. Faith is doing the best we can with what we have. Not changing realities.

When my husband Bill was sick, I said the Serenity Prayer every day: "God, grant me the serenity to accept the things I can't change, the courage to change the the things I can, and the wisdom to know the difference."

What a relief to realize that I was not the Master of the Universe. And what a comfort to have God's presence with me as I came to accept the fact that my husband was dying. This is what bolstered me as we went through the challenging process of facing his diagnosis.

When you get a serious diagnosis and face your darkest day... it is time to ask yourself the important questions.

How much pain can you or your loved one tolerate? There are side effects to all medicines and medical procedures. Do you or does your loved one really want to be in the hospital at the end of life? Or would you/they rather be at home spending their last days surrounded by loving family and friends, and in God's care?

---

2. Hymn by David Haas based on Psalm 46:10, Isaiah 43:1 and John 14:27.

Dr. Eric Topol, a cardiologist and professor at Scripps Research Institute, wrote an article called, "The Smart-Medicine Solution to the Health-Care Crisis" for *The Wall Street Journal* in July, 2017.[3] In the article, he mentions some frightening statistics:[4]

- **1 in 4 patients are harmed while in the hospital.**
- **More than 12 million serious diagnosis errors occur each year in America.**
- **There is a positive response rate of just 25% for patients taking the top 10 prescription medications in gross sales.**

Ask your doctors to quantify the outcomes to the treatment they are recommending. What are the unintended consequences? Get the facts, not false hope. Consider what can happen to you or your loved one in intensive care.

Atul Gawande, physician and author of the critically acclaimed book *Being Mortal: Medicine and What Matters in the End*, writes about what it is really like to die in the ICU:

"In the ICU, you lie on a ventilator, your every organ shutting down, your mind teetering on delirium and permanently beyond realizing that you will never leave this borrowed, fluorescent place."

Dartmouth Hitchcock Medical Center Director of Palliative Care Dr. Ira Byock has worked with patients who, like all of us, could not have imagined anything worse than losing their loved one to a terminal illness. Yet there is something worse than that.

---

3. Topol, MD Eric https://www.wsj.com/articles/the-smart-medicine-solution-to-the-health-care-crisis-1499443449

4. https://www.healthaffairs.org/doi/abs/10.1377/hlthaff.2016.1627?journalCode=hlthaff

"There is having them die badly, suffering as they die," says Dr. Byock. "And maybe the only thing worse than that is looking back and realizing in retrospect that much of their suffering was unnecessary."

Six months after the death of loved ones who spent their last weeks of life suffering in the ICU, their caregivers were three times as likely to suffer major depression, according to Dr. Byock.

How did our society get this way? Why is it so hard to face death?

"We make death harder than it has to be," says Dr. Byock.

Yes, we do. We do not want to lose our loved ones, so we hold on desperately, and we "do everything we can." Of course we do. But this often means chemotherapy, IVs, and other life support. Is this the best way to help those we love who have a terminal illness? In the ICU, the end comes noisily and encumbered by tubes and machines – there is often no chance for you to have said goodbye or "It's O.K." or, "I'm sorry," or "I love you."

Kaiser Permanente Care Management Institute Director Dr. Daniel Johnson, a palliative care physician, says that patients are reluctant to speak up when they've had enough painful or intrusive medical interventions. "They're nervous about what their doctors and their families might think," Dr. Johnson says.

"What they may actually want to say is that I've lived a really good life, and now I want to spend time with my family – instead of the dialysis machine."

Kaiser Care Management Institute Director, Dr. Daniel Johnson

Dr. Gawande, in an interview with NPR's "Fresh Air" Host Terry Gross, said that physicians are hesitant to tell patients there is nothing else they can do, even if statistics show their procedure is unlikely to work. Gawande says sometimes doctors are unable to face the fact of imminent death. Dr. Byock offers a surprising reason for this–and a reason for telling patients the truth:

"The open secret among clinicians is we really care about the people who are our patients... in fact, we hate to make people cry. I've seen so many good doctors who are reticent to tell somebody that their disease is incurable... I know, because I've been doing this for a long time, that clarity, although it may cause acute grief, is actually a gift in this sense, and it's the right thing to do."

It is very hard for families, whose fears and protestations are almost constant while caring for terminally ill loved ones. I know how hard it is, I cared for my husband Bill for 8 years as his health slowly deteriorated. I was afraid, too. But I knew I had the love of God to keep me company and give me strength.

We need to realize this is about quality of life, until the end of life. Don't we want the love of God right there with us? Don't we want comfort and the love of family and friends?

Dr. Gawande cites patient surveys that show the top priorities of people with terminal illness are:
1. **Avoiding suffering**
2. **Being with family**

3. Having the touch of others
4. Being mentally aware
5. Not being a burden to others

Dr. Gawande is spot on when he says,

"Our system of technological medical care has utterly failed to meet those needs."

Doctors who face their own mortality have a different perspective because they know the facts and the limits of medicine.

In a *New York Times* article, "How Doctors Die: Showing Others the Way," there is a poignant story about Dr. Elizabeth D. McKinley, who had terminal breast cancer. She knew she was going to die, and she didn't want any more chemotherapy. She told her loved ones that what she wanted was "a little more time being me and not being somebody else."

So, she turned down more treatment and began hospice care, "the point at which the medical fight to extend life gives way to creating the best quality of life for the time that is left."

"Isn't there some treatment we could do here?" Dr. McKinley's mother pleaded with her son-in-law, also a doctor. But Dr. McKinley and her husband were looking at her disease as doctors who know the limits of medicine; her mother was looking at her daughter's cancer as a mother, *clinging to the promise of medicine as limitless.*

**Entering hospice care is
"the point at which the medical fight to
extend life gives way to creating the best
quality of life for the time that is left."⁵**

We all have our stories of friends and loved ones. You know mine about my husband Bill. Here is another story that may help you determine when hospice is right for you or your loved one.

My friend Ed was 95. He was very ill and had spent weeks in various hospital beds. He was in pain and wanted no more procedures. He begged me to help him. He knew my husband had died peacefully in hospice care. I asked Ed if he was ready to have hospice care. When he nodded, I went off to find the doctor since only a doctor can write hospice orders. I had trouble finding the right doctor, but I persisted.

Finally, in walked a young Chinese doctor with a determined look. He said, "I have been reading this patient's very long medical history. He has been at the hospital often and was just discharged two days ago. It is time to write hospice orders." The doctor said,

**"What is wrong with American hospitals?
The word death is never mentioned here."**

When you get a serious diagnosis and you are navigating the medical system, what you need is realistic advice and counsel from doctors and spiritual support from a trusted minister or a hospital chaplain. When my Bill husband was

---

5. Dan Gorenstein, *The New York Times,* "When Doctors Die: Showing Others the Way," accessed at http://www.nytimes.com/2013/11/20/your-money/how-doctors-die.html

dying, we needed spiritual lifelines as we weighed our medical and palliative options. But what we got instead was this: a chaplain who said, "I am here to accompany him, not to guide him."

My husband had a cluster of increasingly debilitating aging issues. We needed guidance, not company! This is absolutely unacceptable. If clergy are not going to bring God in when we need Him most, our modern politically correct culture has gone too far. Our PC agenda is to avoid offending anyone. Well, in the process, we are disconnecting ourselves from reality. No one wants to bring up death, so patients are suffering in fearful solitude.

Compounding the problem, hospital chaplains - and even hospice chaplains – often avoid talking about death and do not share a God-centered perspective.

When even clergy hesitate to talk about dying and do not mention God, patients and their families suffer through their most challenging and painful times without hope.

Beyond a reluctance to talk about the elephant in the room, there is a serious gap in the training and education of clergy and hospital chaplains. According to the Journal of Palliative Medicine, "Many faith leaders are uncertain of when aggressive treatments should be traded for hospice care and confused about what palliative treatments consist of."[6]

The Journal of Pain and Symptom Management cites a study showing that 70% of clergy members think it is important for

6. Sanders Justin J et al, Journal of Palliative Medicine. October 2017, 20(10): 1059-1067. https://doi.org/10.1089/jpm.2016.0545

them to "encourage ongoing treatment for a cancer patient, even when a doctor says there is no hope for a cure."[7]

Clearly, there is an urgent need for education of clergy and hospital chaplains on end-of-life care issues.

Fortunately, Harvard University's Initiative on Health, Religion and Spirituality is developing a model program called the National Clergy Project, a free course on illness and dying that will emphasize the important role religion often plays at the end of people's lives, and will empower faith leaders to engage their patients in meaningful discussion about their choices at the end of life. The goal of the course is to inform clergy about medical options so that they can offer guidance while patients make their decisions.[8]

This is a crucial development. 75% of clergy are open to such training, according to recent research.[9] We all need to anchor on hope. What our minister or hospital chaplain says to us makes an enormous difference in how we experience the end of life.

If clergy can help us see our condition clearly, to realize that it may no longer be realistic to hope for a cure and, instead, we are facing weeks or months of painful and fruitless treatment, then

---

7. Journal of Pain and Symptom Management, accessed at: http://www.jpsmjournal.com/article/S0885-3924(06)00273-9/pdf

8. Harvard University, The National Clergy Project, accessed at https://projects.iq.harvard.edu/rshm/national-clergy-survey-health-care-end-life

9. Journal of Palliative Medicine study, accessed at https://projects.iq.harvard.edu/files/rshm/files/seeking_and_accepting_pdf.pdf

we can be open to hospice care. Now we can focus on comfort and pain relief, and prepare ourselves for a graceful exit. What a relief!

Hospice care switches the script. We can stop talking about painful and intrusive medical interventions.

Instead, when we accept that the end of life is here, we allow for honest conversations. The end of life becomes a time of intense love and growth. A time to relish your relationships.

A time to say good-bye.

Make the most of your time. Know you have choices. Ask questions along the way. And don't be afraid of letting go, because God is here for you.

We are all dealt different hands in life and in approaching death, but knowing the rules helps. In the next chapters,

I will guide you through the process of a Graceful Exit.

When the caterpillar
thought the world was over . . .

. . . it became a butterfly.

CHAPTER 2

DEATH IS A SPIRITUAL JOURNEY

Change Your Perspective through Faith

"When the caterpillar thought the world
was over it became a butterfly."
- English Proverb

In the first chapter, we faced "the elephant in the room." As caregivers, we cannot fight Father Time. When our loved one is dying, we must face that reality. We do not want to prolong suffering, and we desperately want to do the right thing. But we are afraid.

When we are surrounded by medical experts and life-extending technology, all we can see is a set of physical symptoms to fix: fluid in the lungs, an inability to swallow. We cannot see that the body is shutting down. Oxygen tubes and IVs are blocking a graceful exit, which is to let our loved one depart life in a peaceful way.

We must realize that "doing everything" for our loved ones in the end means that we must be sure they get care for the body, of course, but more importantly, for the soul. We need to look beyond the earthly horizon.

**We need to anchor on God's promise:
"Do not be afraid, for I am with you."**

Isaiah 41:10

Facing death is frightening for many of us. Who can we turn to when our intense fear of death makes us want to fight and deny that death is imminent, or freeze and be unable to act? We may want to cling to our doctors, and fight for a sense of control over the disease. But certainty is impossible. Only faith and trust remain. Why?

Because the alternative is a lonely, fearful place. Nihilists find no meaning in life.

As the wise psychologist Eric Erikson said,

**"It is a terrible thing to be without
basic trust in the universe."**

So, how will we find comfort and peace for ourselves and for our loved ones at this terribly painful time? We need to find support and anchor on God's promise: "Do not be afraid, for I am with you."

Reverend Jamie Haith says:

"We all need support. Fear of death can only be overcome by love. The love of a community that cares for the person as well as a deeper, spiritual love that appreciates that there is more to this life than the here and now."

We caregivers must learn to seize such spiritual lifelines. Reaching out to family and friends, sharing the truth about our loved one's condition, can bring us immense comfort and support that we need, every single day.

We also need to nurture our faith that there is something larger than ourselves guiding us and giving depth to our experience on earth and beyond. I believe that faith is trust in a world that has meaning and loving kindness. The great paradox is that good and evil coexist, and we can get a dire diagnosis, yet live in loving community until we die.

**I believe that faith is trust in a world that
has meaning and loving kindness.**

Spirituality does matter. According to a National Institutes of Health (NIH) research paper, 212 published studies evaluating the effects of spiritual practices such as prayer on health showed that 75% experienced a positive effect, including improved quality of life at the end of life, better coping skills, less anxiety, and less depression.[10]

We must focus on the next chapter. If we can open our minds to the idea that in death, there is Peace at Last, then we can find hope. If we can begin to have conversations with people of faith about what we believe happens after death, we will find great comfort in understanding that dying is a spiritual journey.

How do we find such hope when we feel alone and lost in our hospital room, in the middle of the night? This is the very question that sparked The Hope Initiative. It is my mission to offer spiritual lifelines in every hospital room via closed-circuit TV. If someone is crying out in the middle of the night, and wants desperately to know, "What is next? Where do I go when I die?" I want that person to be able to turn on the TV and find faith-

---

10. Journal of Palliative Medicine study, accessed at https://projects.iq.harvard.edu/files/rshm/files/seeking_and_accepting_pdf.pdf

based answers on behalf of all world religions. I want to offer the very same spiritual lifelines that I have found so helpful and sustaining, to everyone.

Reverend Jamie Haith believes in this mission, too. He has sat with many patients who felt deeply afraid and needed hope. When his father was ill and dying in his hospital bed, Jamie asked him where he was in his faith. His father answered, "Firmly on the fence."

Jamie said to his Dad, "The thing is, when you hear a knock at the door, you don't know 100% who is there, you just open it to see. To me, faith is not so much about knowing as wanting. Do you want Jesus to come in, Dad? Do you want the love of God for yourself?"

"Yes," his father answered. And they cried together in his hospital room.

To watch his father receive love, to see God take away some of his fear, was something Jamie will always be grateful for.

"For this phase of life more than any other, we need more love," Jamie says. "The question is, where can we go to be refreshed by that love? We need to go to the source: God is Love. God loves you totally and he loves you outrageously; he can also fill you with love for others and empower you with it. Especially when we are caring for others we need that refreshment and that power."

If we can talk with our minister or our friends who have a faith; if we ask the important questions, "What happens when we die? Where do our loved ones go?" we will find hope.

When we acknowledge the possibility of Heaven, then we can begin to reframe how we talk about death.

If we think of impending death as a spiritual journey, we can think about how best to soothe our loved one and prepare him or her for that journey.

Is Heaven real?

Thousands of people have had glimpses of Heaven during a near death experience. Dr. Raymond Moody recorded his patients' and many others' experiences in the book *Life After Life*. This was the groundbreaking study of 100 people who experienced "clinical death" and were revived, and who tell, in their own words, what lies beyond death. Today, there are many similar accounts, such as *Heaven is Real*, which tells the story of the little boy whose appendix burst, and who came back from a near death experience recalling a great-grandfather and a sister he had never met.

To me, the most compelling book about the possibility of an afterlife is *Proof of Heaven* by Dr. Eben Alexander, a neurosurgeon who had no belief in God or Heaven until he went into a coma and saw and spoke with a Divine source. Alexander's story is not a fantasy. Before he underwent his journey, he could not reconcile his knowledge of neuroscience with any belief in Heaven, God, or the soul. In his book, Dr. Alexander writes that "true health can be achieved only when we realize that God and the soul are real and that death is not the end of personal existence but only a transition."

Whether or not you believe these stories of experiencing Heaven, the important thing is to find people you can talk with about how God can comfort you now.

Saint Mother Teresa was once asked to pray for clarity, by someone who had traveled far to seek her wisdom. Mother Teresa responded,

"Clarity is the last thing you are clinging to, and must let go of. I have never had clarity; what I have always had is trust. So I will pray that you trust God."

What does it mean to trust God? How will God relieve us of the burden of pain and loss? God will stay with us. That I know. When my husband was dying, I needed to feel near God, and so I talked with Him. I prayed constantly. I formed a relationship with God that made me feel more at ease, more confident, and even joyful at this difficult time in my life. I felt deeply loved and that love sustained me.

I learned that sometimes the best we can do is to sit with our loved ones. They are going through a deeply meaningful time, if only we would stay awhile and listen.

We need to settle our own anxieties so that we can be present for them, to hear where they are in their journey toward the end of their lives.

My co-author and friend Adrienne Hand had an experience with her father that she didn't fully understand until after he died. Her father would pace every day, as if looking for someone, or something. Several times he asked, "Can you lift me up?" Adrienne and her siblings tried to comfort him, but didn't know quite how. Their father didn't say more about it. Later, they realized he was speaking to God. He was ready to be lifted up to be with the Lord whom he had faithfully spoken with throughout his life.

As this prayer so beautifully says,

"Lift us up, God, that we may see further; cleanse our eyes that we may see more clearly; draw us closer to you that we may know ourselves nearer to you."

A friend of Adrienne's told her a similarly poignant story. He said his mother was ready to die, and she asked him to help her cross the threshold. So he said to her,

"You have made your decision; the Angels of the Lord are here."

She was 89 and had suffered long enough with cancer. She had decided to stop chemotherapy, enter hospice, and to ease her pain with morphine. So her son sat by her bedside and held her hands, and they prayed together, saying, "Dear God, I've come to the end of my days. I've had the cancer. I'm ready to come to Heaven. Will you take me?"

They were listening to soothing Vespers and Taizé music while they prayed. She closed her eyes and they both waited. After a while, she opened her eyes, looked at him, and said, "How come I'm still here?" They had a laugh together and then he said, "God must be busy right now."

How wonderful that they could actually enjoy their last moments together this way! He had prepared a loving, graceful exit for her, and accompanied her on her spiritual journey to her loving God.

Even if you don't have a strong faith, take comfort in the words:

"Bidden or not bidden, God is present."

If you would like to learn more about the transition that we all make when we die, or if you would like more support for you and your loved one, you can look into The Hope Initiative, or reach out to the facilitator, Reverend Jamie Haith, by email to hello@htc.us.

And please get the comfort care you deserve. See your pastor or minister, consult with palliative care in the hospital, or seek hospice for the hospital or home through VITAS at https://www.vitas.com/

For ongoing support, you can log in to the Facebook group **Journey of the Soul: Peace at Last**. This site aims to provide patients and their families with spiritual and practical lifelines through uplifting articles and 24/7 streaming webcasts. Our goal is to provide meaningful information – both truthful and hopeful.

This website is a product of a conference that I organized at the National Cathedral in Washington, D.C. Journey of the Soul: Peace at Last brought together doctors, nurses, spiritual leaders from a variety of faith communities, and caregivers who were on this journey with their loved ones. The program offered families comfort – but not false hope – as they faced the truth of a poor prognosis. It also offered resources, both spiritual and human, to help them face reality and manage anxiety. Doctors and nurses offered advice on what it means to "do everything one can" for loved ones.

Dr. Bernie Siegel was the keynote speaker for the conference. In his book, *Love, Medicine & Miracles*, he writes, "Spirituality means the ability to find peace and happiness in an imperfect world, and to feel that one's personality is imperfect but acceptable. From this peaceful state of mind come both creativity and the ability to love oneself, which go hand in hand. Acceptance, faith, forgiveness, peace and love are the traits that define spirituality for me. "

God is the one who fully understands. We are truly not alone! We can anchor on love, hope, and faith in our deep beliefs. I feel at peace with God.

MONA HANFORD

We are truly not alone!

Quite simply put, God offers the optimist possibilities. The pessimist is all dressed up and has nowhere to go.

Live in the moment.

Spend time with those who love you.

CHAPTER 3

FIVE WISHES

Leave a Legacy of Hope

*Death is a 'when' question, not an 'if'
question. So prepare.*

When we come to understand dying as a spiritual journey, we can begin to prepare for this last phase of life in a loving way. We want to bring in as much support and guidance as we can. And we want to comfort and soothe our loved ones.

This is the time for conversations with your doctor and with your minister or spiritual advisor. Your doctor can help you and your loved one make wise choices regarding treatments and medical interventions, and discern which might prolong suffering or diminish quality of life. And your minister can help ease any fears and concerns you may have about dying.

These conversations are crucial to our peace of mind. God is with us! Let us trust Him.

God does not want us to suffer.

There are many decisions we can make that will bring us and our loved ones comfort and solace. I know this can be a daunting

~ 23 ~

prospect. Family members do not like to talk about dying, and yet so often the person who is dying is desperate for this conversation!

How do we even begin?

The very best guide I know for this process is *Five Wishes* living will. *Five Wishes* is known as the first living will with heart and soul, because it considers the personal, emotional, and spiritual needs of the patient above and beyond their medical needs.

What I love about *Five Wishes* is that it is a spiritual guide to our conversations about this stage of life. It was inspired by the work of Saint Mother Teresa in a hospice she ran in Washington, D.C. James Towey worked alongside her there, and developed *Five Wishes* to help families plan ahead and cope with serious illness. James wrote it with the help of the American Bar Association's Commission on Law and Aging, and leading experts in end-of-life care.

Five Wishes is very easy to use. You can sit down with your loved one and fill out the document together. Ideally, this is done well before you or your loved one is incapacitated by illness. I advocate that we all do this in our 50s or 60s, when we are relatively healthy! This is when we can decide who we would like to make health care decisions for us if we are not able to.

If you find yourself in the hospital, however, as long as you or the person who is ill can participate, you can fill it out together.

The *Five Wishes* document covers five areas of concern that we all have when we think about the end of life:

1. **Who do I want to make medical decisions for me when I cannot?**
2. **What kind of medical treatment do I want, or do I want to avoid?**
3. **How comfortable do I want to be?**
4. **How do I want people to treat me?**
5. **What do I want my loved ones to know?**

What do I want my loved ones to know?

This truly is a Godsend, because when we fill out *Five Wishes*, everyone knows exactly what our loved one wants to be done medically, and what he or she does not want. So we don't have to guess! We can be by their side, and follow their instructions for pain relief, comfort, and spiritual connection.

A sample of the *Five Wishes* document is reproduced for you in this book, courtesy of the non-profit group Aging with Dignity. To fill out your own copy, *Five Wishes* is available for a small fee from the website agingwithdignity.com.

When you have your *Five Wishes* in place, it is critically important to let the doctors know it is completed and make sure it is included in your loved one's medical chart. One in three adults has an advanced care directive expressing their wishes for end-of-life care.[11] Yet up to 80% of physicians do not know that document exists![12]

Along with understanding what our loved one wants at the end of life, we also want to encourage him or her to consider what kind of legacy they would like to leave behind. I'm not talking about financial gifts; I'm speaking of a different legacy. A Legacy of Hope.

When we have faced the reality that death is near, and we seek peace of mind by bringing God into the room, we are preparing our Legacy of Hope. We are showing our families that God is with us when we need him most. To accept our death without fear is to give our families the gift of trusting God. This is a Legacy of

---

11. Pew 2006, AARP 2008

12. Yung, VW et al, Journal of Palliative Medicine 2010;13(7): 861-867

Hope that will sustain them. As we face our darkest challenges, we need to know this. The most important thing we leave behind is our faith. This is our parting gift to our families, neighbors, and friends.

Psalm 23 says, "Yea, though I walk through the valley of the shadow of death, I will fear no evil."

To accept our death without fear is to give our families the gift of trusting God. This is a Legacy of Hope that will sustain them.

When we are gone, it is this Legacy of Hope, along with our kindness and good works, that are dearly remembered. You do not need to leave big ticket items to your loved ones for them to feel your love.

One man took the time to make a video of himself taking care of things around the house that would need to be done after he was gone. He left a practical legacy to help his family when they could no longer ask him how to fix something. He wanted to be sure everyone was taken care of in his absence.

My editor Adrienne has a comforter that was her father's. It is meaningful to her because she saw him make his bed every day, with pride and purpose. She saw him kneel before his bed every night and ask for God's grace. Now that he is gone, when she wraps herself in the comforter at night, she feels his presence. Nothing could be more meaningful than that.

"Listen, oh drop, give yourself up without regret, and in exchange, gain the ocean."

Rumi

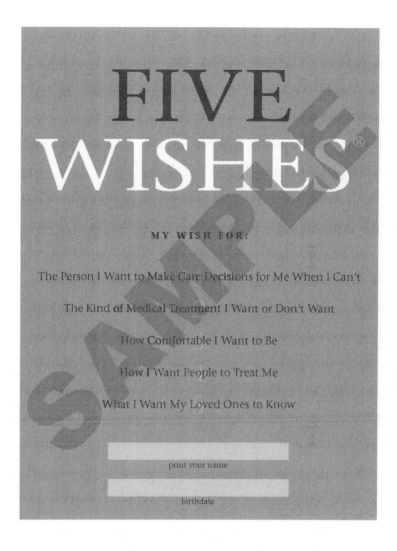

Five Wishes is reproduced here courtesy of Aging with Dignity, all rights reserved.

To fill out your own *Five Wishes* document, please go to www.agingwithdignity.org

Five Wishes

*T here are many things in life that are out of our hands. This Five
Wishes document gives you a way to control something very
important—how you are treated if you get seriously ill. It is an easy-to-
complete form that lets you say exactly what you want. Once it is filled out
and properly signed it is valid under the laws of most states.*

What Is Five Wishes?

Five Wishes is the first living will that talks about your personal, emotional and spiritual needs as well as your medical wishes. It lets you choose the person you want to make health care decisions for you if you are not able to make them for yourself. Five Wishes lets you say exactly how you wish to be treated if you get seriously ill. It was written with the help of The American Bar Association's Commission on Law and Aging, and the nation's leading experts in end-of-life care. It's also easy to use. All you have to do is check a box, circle a direction, or write a few sentences.

How Five Wishes Can Help You And Your Family

• It lets you talk with your family, friends and doctor about how you want to be treated if you become seriously ill.

• Your family members will not have to guess what you want. It protects them if you become seriously ill, because they won't have to make hard choices without knowing your wishes.

• You can know what your mom, dad, spouse, or friend wants. You can be there for them when they need you most. You will understand what they really want.

How Five Wishes Began

For 12 years, Jim Towey worked closely with Mother Teresa, and, for one year, he lived in a hospice she ran in Washington, DC. Inspired by this first-hand experience, Mr. Towey sought a way for patients and their families to plan ahead and to cope with serious illness. The result is Five Wishes and the response to it has been overwhelming. It has been featured on CNN and NBC's Today Show and in the pages of *Time* and *Money* magazines. Newspapers have called Five Wishes the first "living will with a heart and soul." Today, Five Wishes is available in 27 languages.

MONA HANFORD

Who Should Use Five Wishes

Five Wishes is for anyone 18 or older — married, single, parents, adult children, and friends. More than 19 million people of all ages have already used it. Because it works so well, lawyers, doctors, hospitals and hospices, faith communities, employers, and retiree groups are handing out this document.

Five Wishes States

If you live in the **District of Columbia** or one of the **42 states** listed below, you can use Five Wishes and have the peace of mind to know that it substantially meets your state's requirements under the law:

Alaska	Illinois	Montana	South Carolina
Arizona	Iowa	Nebraska	South Dakota
Arkansas	Kentucky	Nevada	Tennessee
California	Louisiana	New Jersey	Vermont
Colorado	Maine	New Mexico	Virginia
Connecticut	Maryland	New York	Washington
Delaware	Massachusetts	North Carolina	West Virginia
Florida	Michigan	North Dakota	Wisconsin
Georgia	Minnesota	Oklahoma	Wyoming
Hawaii	Mississippi	Pennsylvania	
Idaho	Missouri	Rhode Island	

If your state is not one of the 42 states listed here, Five Wishes does not meet the technical requirements in the statutes of your state. So some doctors in your state may be reluctant to honor Five Wishes. However, many people from states not on this list do complete Five Wishes along with their state's legal form. They find that Five Wishes helps them express all that they want and provides a helpful guide to family members, friends, care givers and doctors. Most doctors and health care professionals know they need to listen to your wishes no matter how you express them.

How Do I Change To Five Wishes?

You may already have a living will or a durable power of attorney for health care. If you want to use Five Wishes instead, all you need to do is fill out and sign a new Five Wishes as directed. As soon as you sign it, it takes away any advance directive you had before. To make sure the right form is used, please do the following:

- Destroy all copies of your old living will or durable power of attorney for health care. Or you can write "revoked" in large letters across the copy you have. Tell your lawyer if he or she helped prepare those old forms for you. *AND*

- Tell your Health Care Agent, family members, and doctor that you have filled out a new Five Wishes. Make sure they know about your new wishes.

WISH 1

The Person I Want To Make Health Care Decisions For Me When I Can't Make Them For Myself.

*I*f I am no longer able to make my own health care decisions, this form names the person I choose to make these choices for me. This person will be my Health Care Agent (or other term that may be used in my state, such as proxy, representative, or surrogate). This person will make my health care choices if both of these things happen:

- My attending or treating doctor finds I am no longer able to make health care choices, AND
- Another health care professional agrees that this is true.

If my state has a different way of finding that I am not able to make health care choices, then my state's way should be followed.

The Person I Choose As My Health Care Agent Is:

First Choice Name

Phone

Address

City/State/Zip

If this person is not able or willing to make these choices for me, OR is divorced or legally separated from me, OR this person has died, then these people are my next choices:

Second Choice Name

Third Choice Name

Address

Address

City/State/Zip

City/State/Zip

Phone

Phone

Picking The Right Person To Be Your Health Care Agent

Choose someone who knows you very well, cares about you, and who can make difficult decisions. A spouse or family member may not be the best choice because they are too emotionally involved. Sometimes they are the best choice. You know best. Choose someone who is able to stand up for you so that your wishes are followed. Also, choose someone who is likely to be nearby so that they can help when you need them. Whether you choose a spouse, family member, or friend as your Health Care Agent, make sure you talk about these wishes and be sure that this person agrees to respect and follow your wishes. Your Health Care Agent should be at least 18 years or older (in Colorado, 21 years or older) and should not be:

- Your health care provider, including the owner or operator of a health or residential or community care facility serving you.

- An employee or spouse of an employee of your health care provider.

- Serving as an agent or proxy for 10 or more people unless he or she is your spouse or close relative.

MONA HANFORD

Here is the kind of medical treatment that I want or don't want in the four situations listed below. I want my Health Care Agent, my family, my doctors and other health care providers, my friends and all others to know these directions.

Close to death:

If my doctor and another health care professional both decide that I am likely to die within a short period of time, and life-support treatment would only delay the moment of my death (Choose *one* of the following):

- ❏ I want to have life-support treatment.
- ❏ I do not want life-support treatment. If it has been started, I want it stopped.
- ❏ I want to have life-support treatment if my doctor believes it could help. But I want my doctor to stop giving me life-support treatment if it is not helping my health condition or symptoms.

In A Coma And Not Expected To Wake Up Or Recover:

If my doctor and another health care professional both decide that I am in a coma from which I am not expected to wake up or recover, and I have brain damage, and life-support treatment would only delay the moment of my death (Choose *one* of the following):

- ❏ I want to have life-support treatment.
- ❏ I do not want life-support treatment. If it has been started, I want it stopped.
- ❏ I want to have life-support treatment if my doctor believes it could help. But I want my doctor to stop giving me life-support treatment if it is not helping my health condition or symptoms.

Permanent And Severe Brain Damage And Not Expected To Recover:

If my doctor and another health care professional both decide that I have permanent and severe brain damage, (for example, I can open my eyes, but I can not speak or understand) and I am not expected to get better, and life-support treatment would only delay the moment of my death (Choose *one* of the following):

- ❏ I want to have life-support treatment.
- ❏ I do not want life-support treatment. If it has been started, I want it stopped.
- ❏ I want to have life-support treatment if my doctor believes it could help. But I want my doctor to stop giving me life-support treatment if it is not helping my health condition or symptoms.

In Another Condition Under Which I Do Not Wish To Be Kept Alive:

If there is another condition under which I do not wish to have life-support treatment, I describe it below. In this condition, I believe that the costs and burdens of life-support treatment are too much and not worth the benefits to me. Therefore, in this condition, I do not want life-support treatment. (For example, you may write "end-stage condition." That means that your health has gotten worse. You are not able to take care of yourself in any way, mentally or physically. Life-support treatment will not help you recover. Please leave the space blank if you have no other condition to describe.)

_____

_____

_____

_____

T he next three wishes deal with my personal, spiritual and emotional wishes. They are important to me. I want to be treated with dignity near the end of my life, so I would like people to do the things written in Wishes 3, 4, and 5 when they can be done. I understand that my family, my doctors and other health care providers, my friends, and others may not be able to do these things or are not required by law to do these things. I do not expect the following wishes to place new or added legal duties on my doctors or other health care providers. I also do not expect these wishes to excuse my doctor or other health care providers from giving me the proper care asked for by law.

WISH 3

My Wish For How Comfortable I Want To Be.

(Please cross out anything that you don't agree with.)

- I do not want to be in pain. I want my doctor to give me enough medicine to relieve my pain, even if that means I will be drowsy or sleep more than I would otherwise.

- If I show signs of depression, nausea, shortness of breath, or hallucinations, I want my care givers to do whatever they can to help me.

- I wish to have a cool moist cloth put on my head if I have a fever.

- I want my lips and mouth kept moist to stop dryness.

- I wish to have warm baths often. I wish to be kept fresh and clean at all times.

- I wish to be massaged with warm oils as often as I can be.

- I wish to have my favorite music played when possible until my time of death.

- I wish to have personal care like shaving, nail clipping, hair brushing, and teeth brushing, as long as they do not cause me pain or discomfort.

- I wish to have religious readings and well-loved poems read aloud when I am near death.

- I wish to know about options for hospice care to provide medical, emotional and spiritual care for me and my loved ones.

WISH 4

My Wish For How I Want People To Treat Me.

(Please cross out anything that you don't agree with.)

- I wish to have people with me when possible. I want someone to be with me when it seems that death may come at any time.

- I wish to have my hand held and to be talked to when possible, even if I don't seem to respond to the voice or touch of others.

- I wish to have others by my side praying for me when possible.

- I wish to have the members of my faith community told that I am sick and asked to pray for me and visit me.

- I wish to be cared for with kindness and cheerfulness, and not sadness.

- I wish to have pictures of my loved ones in my room, near my bed.

- If I am not able to control my bowel or bladder functions, I wish for my clothes and bed linens to be kept clean, and for them to be changed as soon as they can be if they have been soiled.

- I want to die in my home, if that can be done.

WISH 5
My Wish For What I Want My Loved Ones To Know.
(Please cross out anything that you don't agree with.)

- I wish to have my family and friends know that I love them.

- I wish to be forgiven for the times I have hurt my family, friends, and others.

- I wish to have my family, friends and others know that I forgive them for when they may have hurt me in my life.

- I wish for my family and friends to know that I do not fear death itself. I think it is not the end, but a new beginning for me.

- I wish for all of my family members to make peace with each other before my death, if they can.

- I wish for my family and friends to think about what I was like before I became seriously ill. I want them to remember me in this way after my death.

- I wish for my family and friends and caregivers to respect my wishes even if they don't agree with them.

- I wish for my family and friends to look at my dying as a time of personal growth for everyone, including me. This will help me live a meaningful life in my final days.

- I wish for my family and friends to get counseling if they have trouble with my death. I want memories of my life to give them joy and not sorrow.

- After my death, I would like my body to be (circle one): buried or cremated.

- My body or remains should be put in the following location_____.

- The following person knows my funeral wishes: _____.

If anyone asks how I want to be remembered, please say the following about me:
_____
_____
_____

If there is to be a memorial service for me, I wish for this service to include the following (list music, songs, readings or other specific requests that you have):
_____
_____
_____

(Please use the space below for any other wishes. For example, you may want to donate any or all parts of your body when you die. You may also wish to designate a charity to receive memorial contributions. Please attach a separate sheet of paper if you need more space.)
_____
_____
_____

THE GRACEFUL EXIT

Signing The Five Wishes Form

Please make sure you sign your Five Wishes form in the presence of the two witnesses.

I, _____, ask that my family, my doctors, and other health care providers, my friends, and all others, follow my wishes as communicated by my Health Care Agent (if I have one and he or she is available), or as otherwise expressed in this form. This form becomes valid when I am unable to make decisions or speak for myself. If any part of this form cannot be legally followed, I ask that all other parts of this form be followed. I also revoke any health care advance directives I have made before.

Signature: _____

Address: _____

Phone: _____ Date: _____

Witness Statement - (2 witnesses needed):

I, the witness, declare that the person who signed or acknowledged this form (hereafter "person") is personally known to me, that he/she signed or acknowledged this [Health Care Agent and/or Living Will form(s)] in my presence, and that he/she appears to be of sound mind and under no duress, fraud, or undue influence.

I also declare that I am over 18 years of age and am NOT:

- The individual appointed as (agent/proxy/ surrogate/patient advocate/representative) by this document or his/her successor,
- The person's health care provider, including owner or operator of a health, long-term care, or other residential or community care facility serving the person,
- An employee of the person's health care provider,
- Financially responsible for the person's health care,
- An employee of a life or health insurance provider for the person,
- Related to the person by blood, marriage, or adoption, and,
- To the best of my knowledge, a creditor of the person or entitled to any part of his/her estate under a will or codicil, by operation of law.

(Some states may have fewer rules about who may be a witness. Unless you know your state's rules, please follow the above.)

Signature of Witness #1 _____   Signature of Witness #2 _____

Printed Name of Witness _____   Printed Name of Witness _____

Address _____   Address _____

Phone _____   Phone _____

Notarization - Only required for residents of Missouri, North Carolina, South Carolina and West Virginia

- If you live in Missouri, only your signature should be notarized
- If you live in North Carolina, South Carolina or West Virginia, you should have your signature, and the signatures of your witnesses, notarized

STATE OF _____   COUNTY OF _____

On this _____ day of _____, 20___, the said _____ and _____, known to me (or satisfactorily proven) to be the person named in the foregoing instrument and witnesses, respectively, personally appeared before me, a Notary Public, within and for the State and County aforesaid, and acknowledged that they freely and voluntarily executed the same for the purposes stated therein.

My Commission Expires: _____

Notary Public

What To Do After You Complete Five Wishes

- Make sure you sign and witness the form just the way it says in the directions. Then your Five Wishes will be legal and valid.

- Talk about your wishes with your health care agent, family members and others who care about you. Give them copies of your completed Five Wishes.

- Keep the original copy you signed in a special place in your home. Do NOT put it in a safe deposit box. Keep it nearby so that someone can find it when you need it.

- Fill out the wallet card below. Carry it with you. That way people will know where you keep your Five Wishes.

- Talk to your doctor during your next office visit. Give your doctor a copy of your Five Wishes. Make sure it is put in your medical record. Be sure your doctor understands your wishes and is willing to follow them. Ask him or her to tell other doctors who treat you to honor them.

- If you are admitted to a hospital or nursing home, take a copy of your Five Wishes with you. Ask that it be put in your medical record.

- I have given the following people copies of my completed Five Wishes:

  _____

  _____

  _____

Residents of WISCONSIN must attach the WISCONSIN **notice** statement **to Five Wishes.**
More information and the notice statement are available at www.agingwithdignity.org or 1-888-594-7437.

Residents of Institutions In CALIFORNIA, CONNECTICUT, DELAWARE, GEORGIA, NEW YORK, NORTH DAKOTA, SOUTH CAROLINA, and VERMONT Must Follow Special Witnessing Rules.

If you live in certain institutions (a nursing home, other licensed long term care facility, a home for the mentally retarded or developmentally disabled, or a mental health institution) in one of the states listed above, you may have to follow special "witnessing requirements" for your Five Wishes to be valid. For further information, please contact a social worker or patient advocate at your institution.

Five Wishes is meant to help you plan for the future. It is not meant to give you legal advice. It does not try to answer all questions about anything that could come up. Every person is different, and every situation is different. Laws change from time to time. If you have a specific question or problem, talk to a medical or legal professional for advice.

Five Wishes Wallet Card

Important Notice to Medical Personnel: I have a Five Wishes Advance Directive.	My primary care physician is:
	Name
Signature	Address _____ City/State/Zip
Please consult this document and/or my Health Care Agent in an emergency. My Agent is:	Phone
	My document is located at:
Name	
Address _____ City/State/Zip	
Phone	

Cut Out Card, Fold and Laminate for Safekeeping

Here's What People Are Saying About Five Wishes:

"It will be a year since my mother passed on. We knew what she wanted because she had the Five Wishes living will. When it came down to the end, my brother and I had no questions on what we needed to do. We had peace of mind."

Cheryl K.
Longwood, Florida

"I must say I love your Five Wishes. It's clear, easy to understand, and doesn't dwell on the concrete issues of medical care, but on the issues of real importance — human care. I used it for myself and my husband."

Susan W.
Flagstaff, Arizona

"I don't want my children to have to make the decisions I am having to make for my mother. I never knew that there were so many medical options to be considered. Thank you for such a sensitive and caring form. I can simply fill it out and have it on file for my children."

Diana W.
Hanover, Illinois

To Order:

Call (888) 5-WISHES to purchase more copies of Five Wishes, the Five Wishes DVD, or Next Steps guides. Ask about the "Family Package" that includes 10 Five Wishes, 2 Next Steps guides and 1 DVD at a savings of more than 50%. For more information visit Aging with Dignity's website, or call for details.

(888) 5-WISHES or (888) 594-7437
www.agingwithdignity.org

P.O. Box 1661
Tallahassee, Florida 32302-1661

Doing everything means . . .

. . . making wise choices so you can
focus on the simple things that bring you joy.

CHAPTER 4

REDEFINE "DOING EVERYTHING"

Palliative Care Brings Us from Fear to Hope

The secret is to assess risk.
Do not live with the illusion that there is no risk.

A ll of us want to do everything we can for our loved ones who are facing a terminal illness. We want the very best treatment at the very best hospital. The more expensive it is, the better it must be. But is the most expensive medical protocol always the most compassionate treatment?

All of us want to do everything we can for our loved ones who are facing a terminal illness.

In this country, medical expenses more than double between ages 70 and 90. The top 10% of all spenders are responsible for 52% of Medicare spending in a given year.[13]

---

13. Medicare Current Beneficiary Survey accessed at https://journalistsresource.org/studies/government/health-care/elderly-medical-spending-medicare

According to Dr. Atul Gawande, "25% of all Medicare spending is for the 5% of patients who are in their final year of life, and most of that money goes for care in their last couple of months - which is of little apparent benefit."

All too often, well-meaning people think they are "doing everything" they can by bringing their loved ones with a terminal illness to the hospital to try every possible treatment. What actually happens, though, is that they end up in the intensive care unit, hooked up to life support and being poked and prodded incessantly.

All too often, well-meaning people think they are "doing everything" they can by bringing their loved ones with a terminal illness to the hospital to try every possible treatment.

Being in the ICU at the end of life is like being in a war zone, and you are losing the war. It is a frightening place.

In her article, "Diary of an Intensive Care Nurse," Kristen McConnell writes:

"Time and again we care for patients who are fighting to die, because in the ICU there are only two ways to die: with permission, too often not granted or granted too late, or in the last ditch fury of a full code blue. We are not helping these people. Instead we are turning them into grotesque containers... reducing their lives to a set of numbers monitoring input and output, lab values and vital signs."

Dixcy Bosley-Smith, a clinical hospice nurse liaison, has seen it all. All too often, patients are released from the hospital too late for hospice care to be helpful. One particularly heartrending case of hers was a 29-year-old woman whose doctor had operated on five of her digestive organs before turning her over to hospice care. She lived two more days.

Where is the boundary? Dixcy says,

"When we have reached the limit of curative capacity, adding surgeries and prolonging treatment only hastens death. There should be an open door to hospice."

Dixcy is absolutely right. When a doctor knows that the extent of disease is so severe that the chemotherapy is not going to prolong life, but only increase pain and perhaps hasten death, it is time for him and for the family to take a leap of faith and enter hospice care. But all too often, the medical system makes that difficult. Doctors are trained to treat every aspect of disease and to persist in the face of obstacles. And even if there is agreement that nothing more can be done for the patient in the hospital, getting discharge paperwork signed and delivered to the patient is very time-consuming and laborious.

Hospital care is helpful when there is hope for a cure. But when that cure is doubtful, when the risks and the pain of further invasive treatment outweigh the possibility of a cure, then it is time to bring in hospice care. Hospice is specialized medical care that treats the mind, body, and soul.

There is no need to wait this long for comfort care. The moment you get a serious diagnosis, you can ask for "palliative medicine." You don't need to wait until you are eligible for hospice. Palliative doctors and nurses focus on relieving suffering while you are getting medical care in the hospital. People who work in palliative care check in with you or your loved one to see how you are doing day to day. They can help you get the care you need, body, mind and spirit. Not all hospitals offer palliative care, but do ask for it.

But when illness has progressed and the impacts of treatment are no longer helping – and instead are diminishing quality of life – this is the time for hospice care. Let's give our loved ones the very best chance at a graceful exit.

The secret is to assess risk and make wise, informed choices. Do not live with the illusion that there are no risks or adverse side effects to urgent care, chemotherapy or other medications, or that these medicines will provide a heroic cure.

In a 2012 research study, 69% of patients with metastatic lung cancer did not understand that chemotherapy is not at all likely to cure their cancer. 81% of those with colon cancer had no understanding of this as well.[14] The researchers on this study concluded:

> **"Chemotherapy remains the primary treatment approach for patients with metastatic lung or colorectal cancer. Although efficacy has improved over time, chemotherapy is not curative, and the survival benefit that has been seen in clinical trials is usually measured in weeks or months. Chemotherapy may provide some palliation, but it is also often associated with substantial treatment related toxic effects."**

All of this obstructs a graceful exit. By the time the patient gets home to the comforts and support of hospice care, he or she is utterly exhausted and depleted. Sadly, in some areas of the country, the average time in home hospice care is five to seven days–or less.

---

14. Weeks, J et al, accessed at http://www.nejm.org/doi/full/10.1056/NEJMoa1204410

How can we turn this around? We need doctors to respect and prolong the quality of our life, not just attack the disease and leave our bodies and souls in shambles. We need to have that conversation with them.

Dr. Joyce Gonin is a Harvard trained nephrologist who believes that doctors must be honest with their patients about their medical condition and then help them alleviate pain and find comfort in their last phase of life. She is inspired by the work and writings of Dr. Elizabeth Kubler Ross, author of the consummate text, *On Death and Dying*.

"When we have exhausted all medical possibilities," Dr. Gonin says, "that's when the tough work begins. It's not 'walk away' it's 'walk toward.'"

Dr. Gonin teaches her students how to deliver the news to their patient that he or she is dying. "First of all," she says, "don't stand at the bed looking down. Sit down eye to eye." If the patient is not conscious, she advises to take the family to a private consultation room and sit down together.

During these conversations, she says, "Listen to the patient and to the family. Hear everything they say. Then comes the hard part: synthesize all of what you heard and bring it back to them with your advice as to how to make all that work, so that your patient has comfort and support."

Dr. Gonin's students know her rules, that there is no such thing as a stupid question or a question asked too often. She tells her patients, "Knowledge is power; the more you understand about your disease, the more you take control and can make decisions to help you." And she lets her patients know when further medical interventions will cause more pain and suffering, to no avail. Dr. Gonin says,

"I tell my students, 'Just because we can do something doesn't mean we should.'"

It is very hard to hear news that you are dying. In Dr. Gonin's experience, she says, "When you give someone bad news, they hear only a tiny fraction." She asks her patients to come back and bring someone, another pair of ears. People process information at their own rate.

Dr. Gonin is a rare physician who takes the time to be present, even when she is not paid to do so. She respects her patients and sees them through to a graceful exit. What she is doing gives me hope. She is from South Africa and brings her perspective to compassionate care. It is often doctors from other countries who recognize the limitations of American idealism and our health care system. Dr. Gonin says,

"Americans believe that death is failure."

This is so true! We don't ever want to admit defeat, or failure. One more treatment, one more opinion will fix everything.

Doctors need to stay with their patients and be honest. One of the main problems with hospital care at the end of life is that you are usually under the care of a stranger; your doctor may have referred you, but he or she is not there managing your care. There is little or no continuity of care, and trust is low. So it is even harder to accept that you are dying.

I am encouraged by the work of Dr. Gonin and others who are focused on compassionate care at the end of life. We need to realize that when we offer our loved one hospice at the end of life, we are doing everything we can.

"Doing everything" means caring not just for the physical body, but for the spirit. It means attending to the dignity of our loved ones, and giving them the chance for a graceful exit.

Yes! We must tend to their spirit! And we need to maintain our own spiritual connection as we care for our loved ones. Unfortunately, many intensive care rooms do not have windows close by. Instead of looking out at the trees and the sunshine, we are looking at a wall of machines. If we cannot see out our windows, we have lost more than fresh air. We have lost the celestial connection. How can we sense the presence of God amid the noise of beeping machines that are blocking our graceful exit?

In hospice care, when we have removed the noisy machines, we can gaze out our windows in peace and sense a connection to a loving God – our most important source of strength. A view of a tree, a courtyard or the sky refreshes our spirit and reminds us of our link to all life and nature.

Hospice care professionals understand this spiritual connection. Some even bring music into the hospital or home to help establish a celestial connection. Music opens a spiritual window.

> **"And it came to pass, when the minstrel played, that the hand of the Lord came upon him."**
>
> **2 Kings, 3:15**

Hospice care at home means . . .

. . . bringing comforting
medications right into your home.

CHAPTER 5

SEEK THE COMFORTS OF HOSPICE

Hospice Can Guide us to a Graceful Exit

This is a deeply spiritual time.

Wwe have talked about facing our mortality and finding the most sensible combination of medical and palliative care. When we can accept that we are dying, we can have precious conversations. This is a profound period of reflection and connection, of finding meaning in the poignancy of the present. It is also a deeply spiritual time that can be expertly guided by hospice.

Dr. Cicely Saunders, who founded the modern hospice movement in the U.S. in the 1940s, said,

"To face death is to face life, and to come to terms with one is to learn much about the other."

Her faith gave her strength which she freely shared with her patients. She said, "We do not know why God has allowed this, but we do know that He will share it; and as He does so He will redeem it and transform it."

Dr. Saunders was the first practitioner to closely observe patients who were experiencing pain at the end of life, to learn what they needed and how best to help.

What is essential, she said, is "really looking (at the patient) ... learning what this kind of pain is like, what the symptoms are like, and from this knowledge finding out how best to relieve them." She advocated strongly for alleviating pain and suffering.

This is the goal of hospice: the management of intractable pain while tending to one's spirit during this delicate transition.

When my dear friend Susan was at home and under the care of hospice, I suggested that we call our minister and together plan a communion service by her bedside and invite her family. Her only child Anne lived several hundred miles away but she immediately accepted the invitation as did her sister and brother, and a dear friend.

To prepare for this special event, with the help of the minister we selected her favorite Bible passages. I brought over my CD player and we played hymns and sang, and she did not want to stop. I had planned on being there for an hour at most as she was weak and tired easily. But the words from the hymns and Bible passages gave her hope. Hope that she was not alone! Hope that God was with us and would be by her side always... She kept wanting to play another hymn. We were together for four glorious hours. The Bible passages and hymns she selected that day we used for the family prayer service by her bedside the next week, and then the family used the same passages and hymns for her funeral.

My friend was able to live in comfort and spiritual grace in her home until the day she died, thanks to hospice care. Hospice treats the mind, body and soul. It is provided by an interdisciplinary care team who offer comfort and support and bring about the best quality of life that can be offered at this very stressful and difficult time.

In hospice care, your loved one can stay in a medical facility or go home. In either setting, hospice supports both the patient and his or her caregivers.

If you are fortunate enough to be home with hospice, your medications and pain relief, including morphine, are provided by hospice. Family or caregivers are educated in when to use each medication. You or your loved one can be situated in the comforts of home, with family and friends nearby, and beloved pets by your side. You can rest in the ease of the familiar.

The fact is, when patients are home with excellent pain relief, they are often vastly relieved to be out of the hospital and they rebound for the last weeks or months of their life. Hospice is the only service that is absolutely dedicated to pain relief at the end of life.

Hospice doctors can prescribe just the right combination of medications to keep you comfortable at home.

Clinical hospice nurse liaison Dixcy Smith says,

"If you can alleviate pain, people feel more in control and want to engage in meaningful conversation. They can say the things they want to say to their loved ones. They can participate in family conversation. They can say goodbye."

When my husband Bill was very ill, I took him to the ER and they asked me to help him to drink a gallon of liquid for a scan. I begged and cajoled him, sip by sip for hours. After all of that, he threw it all up. And the nurse came back with another gallon.

After another 2 hours of torturing him, I gave up. I should have given up after 2 minutes. There is a time for testing when there is a time for cure. And there is a time for comfort and palliative care when hope for a cure is gone. This was his time.

No one tells you that you can get off the treadmill! It was just my gutsy self. But we didn't get off soon enough.

What would have helped us enormously is advice and counsel from a hospital chaplain. We needed spiritual support and guidance as we weighed our medical and palliative options. But all too often, chaplains and even clergy do not offer guidance; instead, in this modern politically correct culture, they say they are "here to accompany patients, not to guide them."

We needed to have honest conversations with our pastor and with our doctor. My family and I spoke with Bill's doctor. Bill's kidneys were failing and dialysis was the next step. He was increasingly disoriented and distressed after his 11-hour surgery.

The hospitalist we spoke with was wise. He told us that Bill's disorientation would make dialysis too stressful for him. He said every day Bill was in the hospital he was going downhill faster. He suggested hospice care in our home. The sooner he got home and back to his known and quiet routine, the better he would be.

"Take him home. It's a sweet place to be."

When we have little time left on this earth, we want it to be good quality time, don't we? Don't we want the comforts of home? Here is a wonderful story that shows how to talk with our doctor about our end of life wishes. A woman named Gay knew she was dying. So she said to her doctor:

"I don't fear death. I have no loose ends. To me death is as natural as birth. I do fear dying. I want to live, but when it is time for me to die I don't want any treatment that will prolong my dying."

Her wise and compassionate doctor responded with words that were enormously comforting to her:

"This treatment may prevent further growth of the tumor. But you can be confident that I understand and respect what you are saying. What you want is what I would want in your situation. Not all my patients do, and I'm fine either way. But I promise you that treatment will end when you want it to. In the meantime, the treatment will improve your quality of life, not degrade it."

Her doctor was true to her word. She treated the tumor and when it was clear that further treatment would diminish the quality of the end of her life, she wrote hospice orders. Gay went home and died in peace one month later, surrounded by her loving family. This is the beauty of hospice.

"The North Star of palliative care is to prevent suffering. If we can give patients exquisite comfort care, we can give them a high quality of life for as long as possible. In my experience, people live longer and with better quality of life in hospice care than they do with extensive procedures near the end of life."
- Clinical hospice nurse liaison Dixcy Bosley-Smith

A wonderful part of hospice care is the quality of people who work in this humane field. The hospice certified nursing assistants I have met are often from the Philippines, Africa, or Central or South America, and they are deeply spiritual and religious. They believe in God and the hereafter - that is why they can do what they do. Often, they bring their Bibles with them and they pray.

VITAS Healthcare is one of the original pioneers of the hospice benefit and today is the largest hospice provider in the country. Their hospice care and palliative services truly give comfort to patients and preserve their dignity in the face of terminal illness. What I like about VITAS is the excellence of their staff. They really care about the people they work with. I have seen VITAS nurses at work and they provide excellent medical care. Adrienne's father was cared for by VITAS nurses who were deeply respectful of his wish to hold on to his dignity as he progressed through the end stages of his life. His hospice nurses brought in beautiful music and prayed with him. When Adrienne's father died, they brought the family yellow roses. It was a gesture and a lasting image she will never forget.

So, if you long for the comforts of home, and you've had enough poking and prodding and noisy machines, ask your doctor or chaplain about hospice care. Your doctor can write you a prescription that brings you home.

Your doctor can write you a prescription that brings you home.

If you cannot get a hospice prescription from your doctor, if he or she says you are not near the end, then get a second opinion. Your doctor may be in denial that you are dying. You need two physicians to sign hospice orders: the attending physician or the hospitalist, who is an expert in taking care of patients in the hospital; and your chosen hospice service medical director. Remember, your quality of life at this stage is most important. You are in charge of your own health care.

Sadly, too many patients do not or cannot get hospice orders from their doctors. Instead, they are discharged to home with no support or comfort medications in place.

**"People are discharged, but if they don't
have the support of hospice they need
at home, they get desperate and come
back to the hospital," says Dixcy.**

Doctors need to face reality and admit when the time has come to end invasive treatment and allow a graceful exit, at home with hospice.

Feel better . . .

. . . brownies can be
infused with medical marijuana.

CHAPTER 6

BE OPEN TO MODERN MEDICINE

Integrative medicine and medical marijuana are helping thousands to relieve pain and suffering.

W hen you get a hard diagnosis, it's a shock to the system. Especially if it is totally unexpected, as in my case. I never saw it coming. But even while I was reeling from the news for a few days, I knew two things were true: God's love was and is right here, and there is more than one way to solve a problem.

Whatever illness you or your loved one are facing, there are many different approaches to healing. We first need to soothe the soul.

I prayed and I gathered my family and friends around me. Then I got to work, researching the best medical and adjunct care - which is known as "complementary" or "integrative" medicine. This can include herbal medicine, cleansing treatments, acupuncture, massage, reflexology, relaxation, counseling services and support groups–and medical marijuana.

Integrative medicine dates back to ancient Sumeria and Egypt. Multiple treatments were combined for the best outcomes. Dr. Sakiliba Mines, Director of the Institute of Multidimensional Medicine in Washington, D.C., says:

"Our bodies have not changed for thousands of years; our livers, brains and all the organs have not increased in capacity to adjust to an environment that (once) was pure but is now saturated with thousands of toxins that (are) carcinogenic."

"Millions of Americans are ill. The American health care system is no longer able to address to chronic diseases in America."

Dr. Sakiliba Mines

Many of us take medications that have side effects. What we may not realize, though, is that combining multiple medicines can be toxic to the body. Integrative medicine practitioners test for this and other hidden syndromes that can show up in digestive problems or other uncomfortable symptoms that many of us simply endure.

I had a consultation with Dr. Mines which I found very helpful. I asked her lots of questions.

For general health and treatment of illness, Dr. Mines recommends an alkaline diet rich in fruits and vegetables so your body can produce minerals like sodium, calcium, magnesium and potassium that help dissolve harmful acids in our systems. "If there are not enough alkaline salts in the blood then acids precipitate in the joints, creating arthritis and gout," Dr. Mines says. She recommends colon hydrotherapy to clear the toxins from the gastrointestinal system that are making us sick.

I asked her why, with all of its apparent benefits, integrative medicine isn't more mainstream.

She said, "Many patients do not have access to integrative medicine because they do not know about it, and when they do, their insurance companies do not cover it. As a result, many patients are discouraged, disappointed and will remain with chronic diseases of which the ultimate cause is unknown. The treatment of their diseases is only masking the symptoms."

I am going to begin therapeutic massage, a healthier diet, more water daily, walks outdoors, and supplemental vitamins and melatonin to help me sleep. All of this makes perfect sense to me. She also said yes to medical marijuana to relieve nausea from my chemotherapy, though she couldn't prescribe it for me since she practices in D.C., where medical marijuana is legal, and I live in Maryland, where it is not. This is a dilemma for many patients, and is the reason many people who are suffering have moved to Colorado and other states where medical marijuana is legally available.

I know many of us have questions about medical marijuana. In this chapter, we will answer those I have heard most often.

How is medical marijuana different from the marijuana that was pervasive in the 1960s – and still is today?

Medical marijuana is not the illegal drug sold on the street. According to the National Council for Aging Care, medical marijuana is derived from the pure cannabis indica plant.

How can it help me or my loved one who is suffering? Is it safe?

Research shows that the part of marijuana known as "cannabinoids," is safe and can be very effective in alleviating neuropathic pain, fibromyalgia, rheumatoid arthritis and relieving muscle spasms caused by multiple sclerosis.[15] Cannabinoids can also be influential as an anti-inflammatory or anti-viral, and to block cell growth and prevent the growth of blood vessels that supply tumors.[16]

The NIH's National Cancer Institute studies show that when sprayed under the tongue cannabinoids alleviate pain in patients with advanced cancer who are not relieved by strong opioids alone.[17]

Cannabidiol (CBD), has been shown to relieve pain, lower inflammation, decrease anxiety, increase appetite and promote sleep without causing the "high" that regular marijuana produces.[18]

I have young friends in college, and I am sure they know more about marijuana than I do. So when I got my serious cancer diagnosis, I checked in with them. When I told them I had never smoked weed, they laughed. They said, "Don't worry, you won't have to smoke it now either. You can get brownies with the critical ingredients."

Wow! I never knew brownies could be so potent. Guess I'm going to be a Hip Granny. So, this is a wonderful development. But is it legal?

---

15. Lynch ME, Campbell F, British Journal of Clinical Pharmacology, Nov 2011 72(5):735-44

16. NIH National Cancer Institute, accessed at https://www.cancer.gov/about-cancer/treatment/cam/patient/cannabis-pdq - section/_3

17. NIH National Cancer Institute, accessed at https://www.cancer.gov/about-cancer/treatment/cam/patient/cannabis-pdq

18. ibid

NIH's National Cancer Institute studies show that two cannabinoids, dronabinol and nabilone, are approved by the FDA to relieve nausea and vomiting that often accompany chemotherapy, for patients who have not responded to opioids.[19]

A growing number of states have enacted laws to legalize medical marijuana. Right now, 28 states, the District of Columbia, Guam, and Puerto Rico allow medical marijuana and cannabis public programs. States permitting medicinal cannabis most often offer treatment to relieve the symptoms of cancer treatment, glaucoma, human immunodeficiency virus/acquired immunodeficiency syndrome, and Multiple Sclerosis.[20]

Still, by federal law, the possession of medical marijuana is illegal in the United States outside of approved research settings - unless your doctor prescribes it. So be diligent and find a legitimate doctor who will help you.

How in the world did we get here? How long has medical marijuana been in use?

The use of marijuana for medicinal purposes dates back at least 3,000 years. It came into use in Western medicine in the 19th century to relieve pain, inflammation, spasms, and convulsions. So this isn't a fad, or a hoax. Medical marijuana is helping thousands.

Integrative medicine is modern medicine. Seek out complementary treatments that will boost your health and give you the gentle, loving care you deserve.

19. ibid

20. NIH NCBI accessed at https://www.ncbi.nlm.nih.gov/pmc/articles/PMC5312634/

Play the cards you've been dealt . . .

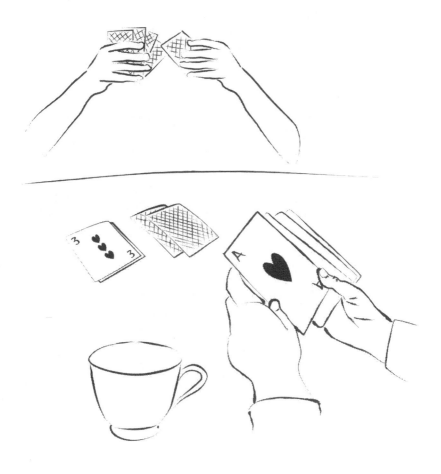

. . . lead with your Ace of Hearts.

CHAPTER 7

PLUG INTO LOVE

Focus on Comfort and Enjoy the Simple Things

Savor the moment

To me, focusing on comfort and enjoying simple things is being open to all the people who have traveled with you on your life's path. In my life, some have been by my side for decades...they are priceless.

Focusing on comfort and enjoying simple things is being open to all the people that have traveled with you on your life's path.

My grandfather was my North Star. He loved me. He was always there with a wise word or a hug. He worked until he was 80 years old. He had arrived in America as an immigrant from Russia on a crowded ship that landed at Ellis Island in New York Harbor. When I was 7, he took me on the Staten Island Ferry and told stories as we went past the Statue of Liberty and Ellis Island.

He was a Russian Orthodox priest and he baptized me, and then decades later he baptized my two children. On our last visit, when grandfather was 84 and had many health problems, my husband and I drove up from New York to Massachusetts to visit him, bring him hugs. He then was living in a monastery. We took him to Howard Johnson's for an ice cream sundae… simple pleasures. As we drove away that day and waved I thought, "You have done your job." I wish I had told him I loved him. But I think he knew. He had always said: "God has given us bodies and minds. Use them and make a difference."

God's love is showing up now through my family, friends and neighbors. My dear neighbor and I have shared many meals together. Decades ago, we would gather for Thanksgiving and Christmas dinner, and the table would be packed with relatives… our husbands, children, grandparents and friends. Now we are widows and we often share a meal and companionship. But when I returned from my surgery, my friend cooked not our favorites, but rather what I needed to replace my blood loss - liver and onions with a side dish of spinach - lots of iron! We laughed a lot, telling stories about how our parents had tried to get us to eat liver when we were children.

Another way I like to spend time is with my grandchildren. One of my granddaughters likes vintage clothes, so we are having fun rummaging in my attic and closets. She is excited to sell these clothes on a hip internet site. But every other outfit she tries on, she has to decide if she wants to sell or keep it. With each outfit there is a story. One dress is my first formal dress that I wore on my first date with her grandfather. Another is my first pantsuit from the late 1960s. It had character: plaid aqua and orange! It was a Christmas gift from my mother-in-law, but when I went to meet my husband at his office, Bill's expression was one of horror. Women just didn't wear pants outside the house, only in the backyard or in casual settings! This story led to lots of laughs about how things have changed. Women could smoke, but pantsuits were on the racy side.

In my life, I have found great inspiration from priests and ministers but also from friends who are homemakers, artists, and even lawyers.

These days, at my bedside, friends are meeting each other for the first time. I have friends who say, "I have known Mona for decades." Other friends say, "Well I have known Mona just a couple of years, but our relationship is deep." The common denominator is that my wonderful friends are passionate in both mind and heart. They care about making this world a better place. They know we have been blessed to have been born in America.

I am grateful to have several friends who call when my knees get wobbly as I face the unknown of this transition. They quote just the right Scripture. One of my favorite passages from the Bible is Romans 8:31-39

"Nothing Can Separate Us from God's Love."

A favorite book that friends read aloud to me these days is *My House Burned Down and Now I Can See the Stars* by Ann Hisle. Now, that's gratitude.

Find your joy. Look through old photo albums with your family. Tell stories that share family history, and stories that make everyone laugh. Looking at old photos brings back happy memories. The other day, my friend and I were looking at a photo of a sandcastle we had spent hours building on the beach with our children. But you could see the clouds on the horizon and soon everything was washed away - and we laughed and laughed because everything was still vivid in our minds.

One of my godchildren recently asked me what he could send me. "Pears from Harry and David?" I said, no, I want a story you remember. Please write one. I'm collecting and enjoying stories.

**What matters to me are the memories
we've shared and the imprints we've
made on each other's hearts.**

So, find your happy memories: books you've loved, old music. Listen to an Elvis concert with someone. Or play a game. Do you remember Monopoly or Dominos, or Old Maid? Pull out your photos and call a friend across the country, share with them the photo you've found that you'll be sending them.

**You can laugh and cry, but always be thankful
for the good times you've shared.**

Put the most important things on the list.

THIS WEEK

- ☑ Have tea with Daughter
- ☑ Lunch with Sam – Friday
- ☑ Invite friends from Church
- ☑ Play cards with grandson

It's all about relationships.

CHAPTER 8

SAY AND DO THE IMPORTANT THINGS NOW

Keep Communication Loving and Open

It's all about love

When we take care of ourselves at the end of life, when we choose hospice care, we have time and space to think clearly and we can create opportunities for meaningful conversations with the ones we love.

Here is what I've said to my children and my friends:

I've loved my life and I want to be here for as long as I can. I've loved the things we've done together. I am stunned, I was flying high. But I am not afraid of moving on.

I love the trips I've taken with all of you over the years - but now I'm about to take another trip. I always knew I would make this journey. My grandfather bought me a ticket when he baptized me. With a little oil and water and a lot of faith, I'm going to collect my inheritance now, and it's my kind of trip. No visas, no luggage, no missed trains.

Thanks for seeing me off on my journey.

Bon Voyage!

P.S. To my children, I just wanted to remind you that my grandfather, your great-grandfather, also bought you tickets when he baptized you. They await.

The best is yet to come!

What you say and how you say it can show your strength and resilience, and give others the rich benefits of your experience. Harvard University Professor Dr. George Vaillant studied resilience, the ability to rebound after the shock of loss or physical injury. He studied over 800 men and women for 50 years and found that our ability to cope - our adaptability, optimism, zest for life - and our ability to give back to the next generation, make our lives deeply satisfying as we age. This is what it means to have a rich, meaningful spiritual life and it is how we can live in loving community. It is also how we take care of ourselves, body, mind and soul.

**Your faith and resilience help
those around you cope.**

In Dr. Vaillant's book *Spiritual Evolution: A Scientific Defense of Faith*, he writes:

"All forms of spiritual healing have in common empathy, healing within a circle of caring persons, permission to feel and express emotions, shared responsibility for pain, and reverence for life rather than for self. Such 'blessings' lower blood pressure, ease pain, relax muscles and postpone death."

Yes, I am facing stage IV cancer, but I am grateful for many things. I'm grateful that friends are coming with lunch and dinner and staying for a visit. It is priceless to get hugs. Several friends and I have talked about others we know who have battled cancer for five, ten, or even 40 years.

Well, I have thought about the battles these wonderful people have gone through, and my take away is, "Aren't I lucky that I was cancer-free for almost three quarters of a century." I have been enjoying a healthy and full life for almost 75 years.

A friend of mine has said, "Leave Mona with lemons and she will try to make lemonade." Well, here I go again, making lemonade.

Honestly! After watching calories all my life, I can now eat that brownie sundae with ice cream whenever I want! And glorious macaroni and cheese!

Enjoy what you can. And savor every bite.

There is a lot of laughter when people visit. My friends and I enjoy each other. When they leave, they say, "I'm coming back." One friend even said, "I'm coming back and I'm bringing my husband. He wants to get in on the fun." Good thing I'm an extrovert, I thrive on the company. It's like 6 antidepressants!

When friends visit, they become part of a loving community. So don't hold back! Visit your friends who are dying. Meet new friends. Share the experience. It is a very special time.

Be playful and optimistic! Go ahead and blow bubbles like we did as children. Watch them float across the room until they pop. How fabulous! This is renewing a sense of wonder. Watching my dogs Ace and Liberty chase squirrels in the backyard has the same effect, they never get bored. It's a wonderful adventure, and we are locked in the joyful moment.

Take special care of yourself or your loved one who is dying. Light scented candles. Enjoy a gentle massage with your favorite scented cream. Listen to your favorite music. Surround yourself with comfort and pictures of your family.

Stay connected with family and friends, and with God – they are your spiritual lifelines! I talk with my loved ones every day. And I talk to God throughout the day. I feel blessed to have such strong and loving family and friends, and to feel God's presence – He is always near me.

As I go through this journey, I've been thinking about how to share what has been meaningful to me. It is so important to give back. I've had a wonderful life and I have much to share.

I've made a list of things to give, and I have chosen gifts that give a message. Not expensive things, but meaningful treasures. The glass bowl and white pebbles that I've always used to grow narcissus bulbs, which are magical. They turn from dried brown bulbs into things that blossom beautifully and smell so good. It's about renewal.

The journals that I've kept… I want others to benefit from my experience; insights I've gained over the years. And my favorite books! Books of fairy tales that show there is both good and evil, and that we need to focus on the good, to search it out. And not to have false expectations.

In *The Witches* by Roald Dahl, my favorite line is, "It doesn't matter who you are or what you look like, so long as somebody loves you."

Books are values to live by and things to cling to when life gets tough. They're all about how to find your way. The books you've highlighted and notated over the years make great gifts. I gave my dog-eared copy of Scott Peck's *The Road Less Traveled* to my granddaughter. *Please Understand Me*, the book about the Myers-Briggs character and temperament test that helps us all understand each other, has been my go-to. We all bring different gifts and we have to work together as a team. *The Seven Habits of Highly Effective People* by Stephen Covey is also a great book. It gets you on the right path with the idea, "begin with the end in mind."

My old records have brought me such joy. Nat King Cole's "Unforgettable." Louis Armstrong's "When The Saints Go Marching In." Frank Sinatra's "You're Nobody 'Till Somebody Loves You." Art Mooney's "I'm Looking Over a Four Leaf Clover." Is that fun? And of course, Frank Sinatra's "Someone to Watch Over Me." Giving these away is giving joy and love.

Gifts do send messages. A candlestick to light your way in dark times. God boxes, small boxes to hold notes about your hopes and fears. In one of my God boxes, my note says, "God, please help me. Let me remember that you are always with me. Help me to accept that things happen 'in God's time' and not to be afraid."

It's these kinds of messages that will resonate for your loved ones for the rest of their lives.

The work that I've done for the past 20 years has been uplifting and sustaining. Now, through The Hope Initiative, I am giving back. This course that we are giving in hospitals and churches for caregivers has been a spiritual lifeline for many. Reverend

Jamie Haith surrounds you with the message of hope, that there is more, that we are not alone.

So, in this special time, keep in touch with your emotions. Remember to avoid instant madness. Be a good navigator. Emotions are your instrument panel. Do not smash or ignore them. When we speak honestly about death, we show our strength and resilience and we help those around us cope.

Say it now. Tell the people you love how you feel.

Now is the time to tell your loved ones, "I love you, thank you. Please forgive me, because I forgive you."

Now is the time to receive cards and letters, emails and phone calls. I like the Art Buchwald model. He selected ten people to speak at his memorial service and asked them to send their remarks to him right away so he could enjoy reading them now.

I'm getting so many messages of love from my dear friends and family. This is a time to feel cherished – because you are.

And though it is hard to say good-bye, picture this as your exit line:

"Dear, I will be just fine and so will you."

This is what courage looks like . . .

"Yea, though I walk through the valley of
the shadow of death, I will fear no evil."

PSALM 23

CHAPTER 9

OPEN THE DOOR TO GOD

*Explore Spiritual Tools Even if You
Aren't Sure What You Believe*

"Bidden or not bidden, God is present."

When we are scared and need courage to face these difficult days, we need to lean on the sustaining Infinite and open the door to possibilities.

**Yea, though I walk through the valley of
the shadow of death, I will fear no evil:
for thou art with me; thy rod and thy
staff they comfort me. - Psalm 23**

Whether you believe in God or Buddha, or you have your own spiritual beliefs, the important thing is to open the door and let in some hope that there is something more than what we see here on earth. I believe there is.

One night, our godson was with us for a family dinner. He had just graduated from college and was bright and engaged in exploring life's big questions. He commented that he could no longer believe in God. It just does not make sense. "If there is a God why do bad things happen?"

My husband, who had a scientific questioning mind, explained how he came to accept the things that do not seem to make sense. "It is really quite simple, PJ. Our dog Count does not understand calculus. Does that mean calculus does not exist? No, it is just beyond his understanding. Well, we are humans and we cannot understand everything about God and the Universe."

PJ came back to visit recently. He is now 50 and he reminded me about how that explanation about the dog and calculus helped him put aside his need to know it all. It helped me to accept God and that, he said, had made all the difference.

I find God in the most unexpected places. I call these God moments. I believe coincidences are God's way of staying anonymous. When I look back on my life I see so many God moments.

People represent God's love to us. In circumstances that are horrific, such as when a child dies, God shows up in the people who surround us and comfort us. I call that God's hand.

It's not that some people have access to God, we all do.

Bidden or not bidden, God is present.

Reverend Jamie Haith was ordained by the Church of England and began his career as a hospital chaplain in central London. Speaking about that time, he says, "It was my privilege to sit with dying and chronically ill people, talk to them, and pray with them in those desperate and painful situations."

As a minister, Jamie offers hope that transcends a natural fear of death. This is so important, because we don't want our fear to be so overpowering that we cannot be present in the here and now, and we can't make decisions about our health care. Jamie says what we need to do is "to step into God's love." We can make the choice to trust that God loves us and our family. He knows what you are going through and he will help you cope. God is good! He has a plan beyond what we can see.

God's love will see you through.

When my mother-in-law was dying at 92, she had been disabled for 12 years. The day finally came when she took to her bed and did not want to get up. The gerontologist came to visit, and suggested that we begin hospice care. We knew that the end was in sight but she was afraid of letting go.

It is easier to let go when you have the glimmer of hope that there is something more. Call it something as general as peace at last, or as specific as Heaven, where family will meet you. Visualize this, as author Henry Van Dyke wrote:

**"I am standing on the seashore.
A ship spreads her sails
to the morning breeze and starts for the ocean.
I stand watching her until she fades
On the horizon, and someone says,
"She is gone."**

**"Gone where?
The loss of sight is in me, not in her.
Just at the moment someone says,
"She is gone,
There are others watching her coming.
Other voices take up the glad shout;
Here she comes."**

Another way of visualizing Heaven is this beautiful story of a father who has died, and whose family imagine he is on his beloved sailboat, sailing across the ocean. When his daughter died, the family visualized their father reaching out his hand to her as she swam toward him, reaching for his hand.

When my husband lay dying in our family room, I leaned on God, knowing it was not all up to me, a mere human. I held his hand and whispered to him,

"The best is yet to come." I accept the mystery of Heaven and trust a loving God.

So do what you can and then climb into God's lap.
As Canon Henry Scott Holland wrote in 1910,

Death is nothing at all

I have only slipped away into the next room

I am I and you are you.

Whatever we were to each other, that we are still.

Call me by my old familiar name,

Speak to me in the easy way which you always used.

Put no difference into your tone,

Wear no forced air of solemnity or sorrow.

Laugh as we always laughed at the little jokes we en-joyed together.

Play, smile, think of me, pray for me.

Let my name be ever the household word that it always was.

Let it be spoken without effort, without the ghost of a shadow on it.

Life means all that is ever meant.

It is the same as it ever was,

There is absolutely unbroken continuity.

What is this death but a negligible accident?
Why should I be out of mind because I am out of sight?
I am but waiting for you, for an interval,
Somewhere very near just around the corner:
All is well.

When facing a transition . . .

. . . be the optimistic twin.

CHAPTER 10

EMBRACE THE NEXT CHAPTER

Release Control and Find Serenity
in the Promise of Peace

So often here on earth we strive to control our circumstances. We think money, power, and education will create Heaven on earth for us. We'll have the perfect life, the perfect body, the perfect house. Well guess what, we cannot control any of it! The good news is that once we give up control of our physical circumstances, our souls move on to peace - true peace - what we've been searching for all our lives.

The reality is, if you believe you can cure all physical problems and never die, you are setting yourself up for failure. Getting well is not the only goal. Even more important is learning to live without fear, and to have peace of mind.

When we open the door to God's love we open
the door to possibilities: less fear, more hope.
Life is a series of hurdles. Whatever happens,
you will overcome with love and faith.

Death is so much better with God's love and mercy. Death need not be feared. We have to trust that God will bring us to the other side, and we have to trust that those we leave behind will find their way with God's help. That is what Peace at Last means.

All transitions require trust because the future is unknown until we get there. The ultimate question is whether you're an optimist or a pessimist.

Consider this story about twins in their mother's belly - one is an optimist and the other, a pessimist. The optimist thinks that when the umbilical cord is cut there will be an exciting new chapter. This twin is open to possibilities. "Maybe we'll learn to talk and walk and hear."

The pessimistic twin thinks that's ridiculous. "How could we live without the umbilical cord? That will be the end of us. No one has come back to tell us there is something else. If there were, we would know. No, it's over."

Today, we encounter the same narrow thinking— many believe that since no one has come back after dying, death is the end. How hopeless to limit our possibilities. Let's be open to possibilities, and the Mystery and Majesty of God!

The optimist still holds out possibilities. He says to his twin, "Maybe there is someone watching over us. Maybe someone's been watching over us all this time. I feel as if we've been cared for and loved."

To this, his twin scoffs, "Impossible. We've been alone all this time and there is no next chapter. This is it."

I prefer to be the optimist. I believe that there is something beyond the earthly horizon. When Christopher Columbus set out to sail "beyond the horizon," most subscribed to the flat earth theory, and there was a certain arrogance in assuming that, because no one had ever met someone who returned from "beyond the horizon," it could not exist. My preference is to be open to God and possibilities rather than to be the pessimist, who refuses to be open to hope. I believe there is something more.

I spend my time in a room with many windows. I look out to my backyard and watch the birds. A bird feeder can provide endless entertainment, but more importantly, it reminds us we are interdependent. We are interconnected. Reach out and embrace the wonder of the world. We set ourselves up for failure if we believe we can cure all physical problems and never die. The most important thing is learning to live without fear, to be at peace with life and, ultimately, death.

Being the optimist, I am a believer. My prayer is,

Dear Lord,
During these uncertain and confusing
times, shine on us and through us, and
remind us that however bad it may seem,
nothing can separate us from you.

Some people visualize faith this way:

One night I dreamed a dream.

As I was walking along the beach with my Lord.

Across the dark sky flashed scenes from my life.

For each scene, I noticed two sets of footprints in the sand,

One belonging to me and one to my Lord.

After the last scene of my life flashed before me,

I looked back at the footprints in the sand.

I noticed that at many times along the path of my life,

especially at the very lowest and saddest times,

there was only one set of footprints.

This really troubled me, so I asked the Lord about it.

"Lord, you said once I decided to follow you,

You'd walk with me all the way.

But I noticed that during the saddest and most trouble-some times of my life,

there was only one set of footprints.

I don't understand why, when I needed You the most, You would leave me."

He whispered, "My precious child, I love you and will never leave you

Never, ever, during your trials and testings.

When you saw only one set of footprints,

It was then that I carried you."

- **Footprints in the Sand**

So now I leave you, my dear readers, and trust that you will find your path toward your own graceful exit. This book is my Legacy of Hope. All will be well.

Heavenly Father, thank you that you are always good and loving. May I have the faith to believe you are with me in every struggle, and the trust to accept that ultimately you are in control. Please empower me with your unfailing love and grant me your wisdom, kindness and strength. Instill a hope of Heaven in me and those I love, that we would know you are always with us.

Amen

Acknowledgments

I am grateful to my family and friends who inspired me to write this book.

Adrienne Hand, my co-author and editor, paid attention to each citation and comma and was a soulmate on this journey. What a blessing to have recruited her to work with me a month before I got my serious cancer diagnosis. It was as if an angel put the thought in my mind. I am also grateful to the talented artist Lalie Tongour, who captured the message of a graceful exit in 10 stunning illustrations and our beautiful cover. She has been on this book journey with me from the beginning. I couldn't have done it without her.

Jamie and Andy Haith, co-leaders of Holy Trinity Church (HTC), offered abundant spiritual guidance and helped me articulate the message of hope for this book. In addition to contributing meaningful passages to the book, and teaching The Hope Initiative course, they also created and produced a video on preparing a graceful exit for YouTube, making this message accessible to all.

I am thankful to Vicki Hart and Sue Ramthun of VITAS for sharing their expertise and helping to spread the message about the immense value of hospice and palliative care. Aging with Dignity, a non-profit organization that safeguards the human dignity of people as they age or face serious illness, gave us permission to publish *Five Wishes* in this book. This compassionate living will is helping thousands to make wise choices at the end of life and to ensure loved ones know their wishes for a graceful exit.

I am also grateful to Don Ottenhoff of the Collegeville Institute for publishing a series of interviews with me called, "Hope at the End." Nancy Palmer shared my story and normalized the taboo subject of death with honesty and hope in an interview for *The Atlantic*. Grant Grissom, Dixcy Bosley-Smith, and Napier Shelton contributed thoughtful content to the book.

Our readers Traci Grigg, Dee Nelson, Grant Grissom and Barbara Rossotti paid close attention not only to the mechanics of the book, but the message.

I'd like to thank Liz Ehinger for years of collecting my source materials for this book in an online library. Chevas Wong of HTC filmed and edited the YouTube video in which Jamie Haith interviewed me about *The Graceful Exit*.

I am grateful to William O'Neill at Latham & Watkins who provided us with advice on copyright authorization, and to Tracey Braun for providing guidance on publication.

Finally, I am deeply grateful to Susan Wojick for editing my writing over the years and for continuing the mission of this book with Adrienne Hand. They plan to start a blog offering hope at the end, the essence of *The Graceful Exit*.

Appendix

"Hope at the End of Life"
An Interview with Mona Hanford

June 12, 2017 By Betsy Johnson-Miller

Mona Hanford is an end-of-life-care activist, teacher and writer. She chaired the conference "Journey of the Soul–Peace at Last," which was held at the Washington National Cathedral. In this interview, she explains her work with the Hope Initiative, a program designed to offer support in hospitals and churches to those facing end-of-life decisions. Mona currently serves on the board of the Collegeville Institute.

What is the Hope Initiative, and what does it seek to do?
It's a course we designed to provide a spiritual lifeline for caregivers and patients who are dealing with serious medical issues. It was my belief that people needed this kind of support as they were caring for family members during that long last chapter, so the Reverend Jamie Haith created a five-part series that includes talks on love, hope, peace, joy, and faith. People can freely access the course at our website, and while the talks do have a Christian focus, the material will help people from all faiths, because it's really about God.

If they can think there's peace at last, then there's hope.
What do you do when the worst thing has happened to the family, when they are losing a loved one? Your aging father fell and broke his hip, and he's 92. The doctors might want to put in a feeding tube, but he's had dementia for the last five years and doesn't even know who anybody is in the family. How do people make decisions in these kinds of situations? We urge people to focus on the next chapter. If they can think there's peace at last, then there's hope. That's why we call this the Hope Initiative. Having God in our lives and having spiritual lifelines that attach us to God's care are so important, because otherwise we are left with the grim reality of looking at the furnace or the dirt. I strongly believe that having a hope that extends beyond death has a significant impact on end-of-life decisions we face either for ourselves or our loved ones.

Why is it important to have this kind of support for people?
People are afraid to face the reality that we all have an expiration date.

So many people are in hospitals doing everything for family members, and by "everything," I mean every procedure, every device, every medication, every test. People are afraid to face the reality that we all have an expiration date. But we do, and so the question then becomes, do we want a graceful exit or a prolonged and possibly painful one? We at Hope Initiative try to offer a big picture and a toolkit to help people make these difficult decisions—to support them and offer them a perspective on the importance of hope. We want to tell them, "Do not be afraid," and give them confidence that they aren't killing their father because they aren't putting a feeding tube in when he's 92 and very sick. What people of hope can admit is that his body is shutting down, and it might be better to let him depart life in a peaceful way. Medical technology frequently ends up being a hindrance rather than a help: people put hope in technology and medications rather than in God.

Do you think most people fear death?
Yes. The bad news is that we all have to face the fact that death is here for each and every one of us. The Hope Initiative is built on the idea that one way to have a graceful exit is to trust God. We can try and block God's time schedule by hooking our loved ones up to lots of machines, but once a person gets tied up to those machines and they are old, they rarely get untied. The person becomes a prisoner. But it doesn't have to be like that. I remember reading an article by a doctor who works in an intensive care unit, and he said something like, you know, if Martians landed and read what we did to patients in Intensive Care, they would say, 'What did those patients do that was so horrible that you are torturing them?'

I am also reminded of another story. A neighbor's brother Joe was a great surgeon and he got stage IV cancer, and they tried a few things, but it was very serious. He decided that he wasn't going to go through any more painful treatments. All of the doctors huddled around him as he was leaving the hospital, and they said, "What are you going to do?" He said, "I'm going home to drink champagne. Come visit me."

The next day a colleague showed up with a case of champagne. Joe had a comfortable 3 months at home reminiscing and looking at photos with family and friends and laughing and praying... a Graceful Exit!

Sometimes, it's more important to make the most of our time here rather than get burned with radiation or poisoned with chemo. There are certainly times for that, but there also comes a time when people have had enough. I want them to feel that God is with them in that moment and will help guide them.

We want to offer them spiritual lifelines and support as they make these difficult decisions.

So one of the things that is very important to you is letting go gracefully?
Yes. At times, what we try to do in hospitals and at the end of life is not appropriate, because of what it's costing financially, and because of what it's doing to the person and their loved ones. But navigating that reality can be difficult for many people. That's why our work at Hope Initiative is so important—we want to offer them spiritual lifelines and support as they make these difficult decisions. We invite those who are facing this reality to be open to the possibility of a graceful exit, which means closing the loop with everybody you love and care about.

What does "closing the loop" look like?
Sharing memories, telling everyone you care about how important they were, saying, "I love you," and "I'll always be with you." I personally want my exit line to be: "I'll be fine, and you'll be fine. We're in God's hands."

Death is so much better with God's love and mercy. We have to trust that God will bring us to the other side, and we have to trust that those we leave behind will find their way with God's help. Death is so much better with God's love and mercy. Death need not be feared. That is what Peace at Last means.

For additional resources or to offer the Hope Initiative to your church or medical facility, please visit the Hope Initiative website. http://htcmosaic.com/hope/

BEYOND THE HORIZON:
A Letter from Mona Hanford

D r. Francis Collins, a physician-geneticist, who serves as director of National Institutes of Health, is noted for his discoveries of disease genes and his leadership of the Human Genome Project. He also believes in God. In his book *The Language of God*, he asserts, "In my view, there is no conflict in being a rigorous scientist and a person who believes in a God who takes a personal interest in each one of us." As the founder of The Hope Initiative, I wholeheartedly agree with Dr. Collins. I have been a caregiver for family and friends, and I have served on the board of trustees of our local hospices, and in so doing, I have witnessed first-hand the need to embrace the many medical cures science provides, while at the same time accepting the limits of those human interventions and the need to trust God.

In every life, there comes a time when we must look "Beyond the Horizon." At that time, real hope requires that we turn to God. Unfortunately, our modern secular culture has removed God from the end-of-life discussion, and in so doing, there have been horrific unintended consequences. Without the presence of God, our thinking is limited to staying on the medical treadmill. Too often patients are tortured until their last breath. Too often a patient's family leaves the hospital after a death suffering not only grief, but also post-traumatic stress.

Without God, talking about death is too grim, and we are left hopeless— are we going to be burned in the furnace, or buried in the dirt? As the founder of The Hope Initiative I want to bring God back into the discussion. Each faith has their own tradition, and I respect all faiths. I am a Christian, so The Hope Initiative has started offering spiritual lifelines from the Christian perspective. My hope is other faiths will add their voices.

In March 2001, I began my efforts by chairing "The Journey of the Soul— Peace at Last," a conference at the Washington National Cathedral. The conference, attended by 1,500 people was sold out, and there were another 500 names on the wait list, so I know there is a hunger in our culture for spirituality beyond our human limits.

Today, as I continue in this work, I feel blessed that The Hope Initiative is offering a faith-based course designed to enable caregivers of the chronically and terminally ill to prepare emotionally and spiritually for the struggles and difficulties of caring for an ill person. The discussions focus on Love, Hope, Faith, Peace and Joy, and how they can provide support during difficult times.

Mona Hanford
Founder of The Hope Initiative

This article is so named because, when Christopher Columbus set out to sail "beyond the horizon," most subscribed to the flat earth theory, and there was a certain arrogance in assuming that because no one had ever met someone who returned from "beyond the horizon" it could not exist. Today, we encounter the same narrow thinking— many believe that since no one has come back after dying, death is the end. How hopeless to limit our possibilities. Let's be open to possibilities, and the Mystery and Majesty of God!

Resources for Preparing Your Living Will

F ive Wishes document is available for a small fee from the non-profit group Aging with Dignity, on the Internet at: http://www.agingwithdignity.org/

Remember, when you have your *Five Wishes* or alternative living will in place, it is critically important to let the doctors know it is completed and that it is in your loved one's chart. If you are in home hospice care, be sure your living will document is visible, taped to the refrigerator or in a file by the front door. 1 in 3 adults have an advanced care directive expressing their wishes for end-of-life care.[21] Yet up to 80% of physicians do not know that it exists.[22]

This is an urgent call to action for enhanced continuity of care from primary physician to hospital at the end of life.

---

21. Pew 2006, AARP 2008

22. Yung, VW et al, Journal of Palliative Medicine 2010;13(7): 861-867

For further information about advance care planning, see the Centers for Disease Control and Prevention article, "Advance Care Planning: Ensuring Your Wishes Are Known and Honored if You Are Unable to Speak for Yourself," available at: www.cdc.gov/aging/pdf/advanced-care-planning-critical-issue-brief.pdf

Caregiver Resources

Websites that connect caregivers to available resources, by state:
- Caregiver.org lists the support groups available to caregivers.
- Eldercare.gov lists the resources available to caregivers.
- The national Alzheimer's Association lists the support groups available to those caring for patients with Alzheimer's disease.
- The American Cancer Society's website cancer.org lists the treatment and support resources available to caregivers and patients.